WORLD
LEADERS

People Who Shaped the World

WORLD LEADERS

People Who Shaped the World

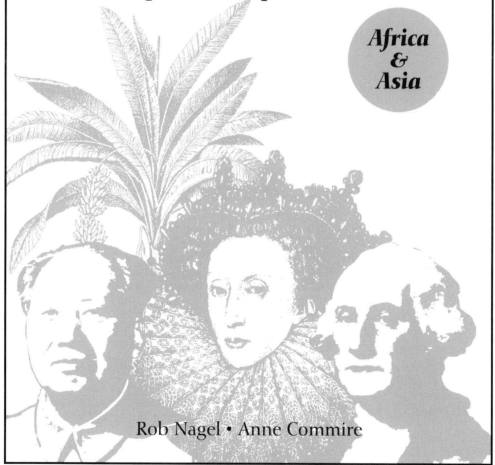

Africa
&
Asia

Rob Nagel • Anne Commire

AN IMPRINT OF
GALE RESEARCH INC.

World Leaders:
People Who Shaped the World

Rob Nagel and Anne Commire

Staff

Sonia Benson, U·X·L *Associate Developmental Editor*
Kathleen L. Witman, U·X·L *Assistant Developmental Editor*
Thomas L. Romig, U·X·L *Publisher*

Mary Kelley, *Production Associate*
Evi Seoud, *Assistant Production Manager*
Mary Beth Trimper, *Production Director*

Pamela A. E. Galbreath, *Cover and Page Designer*
Cynthia Baldwin, *Art Director*

Keith Reed, *Permissions Associate (Pictures)*
Margaret A. Chamberlain, *Permissions Supervisor (Pictures)*

The Graphix Group, *Typesetting*

Library of Congress Cataloging-in-Publication Data
World leaders: people who shaped the world / {edited by} Rob Nagel,
   Anne Commire.
      p.   cm.
   Includes biographical references and index.
   ISBN 0-8103-9768-4 (set)
      1. Kings and rulers --Biography. 2. Heads of state--Biography. 3. Revolutionaries--
   Biography. 4. Statesmen--Biography. I. Nagel, Rob. II. Commire, Anne.
D107.W65 1994
   920.02--dc20   94-20544
                                                                                        CIP
                                                                                          AC

This book is printed on acid-free paper that meets the minimum requirements of American National Standard for Information Sciences—Permanent Paper for Printed Library Materials, ANSI Z39.48-1984.

ISBN 0-8103-9768-4 (Set)

ISBN 0-8103-9769-2 (Volume 1)
ISBN 0-8103-9770-6 (Volume 2)
ISBN 0-8103-9771-4 (Volume 3)

Printed in the United States of America

Published simultaneously in the United Kingdom by Gale Research International Limited (An affiliated company of Gale Research Inc.)

Contents

VOLUME 2: EUROPE

VOLUME 3: NORTH AND SOUTH AMERICA

Preface

Through 120 biographical sketches in three volumes, *World Leaders: People Who Shaped the World* presents a diverse range of historical figures. Many of those profiled are political or military leaders whose achievements have been evident and far-reaching. Others featured may not be as conspicuous to the beginning student of history, but their achievements—considering the social context of the eras in which they lived and the barriers against which they fought—are no less great.

The individuals chosen for inclusion in *World Leaders* fall into one or more of the following categories:

- Those who significantly changed their nation or empire, affecting its—or the world's—course permanently or for a very long time.
- Those who exhibited great qualities in many areas—military, politics, art, religion, philosophy.
- Those who struggled against the forced limitations of gender, race, or social standing to achieve their ideals, leaving a trail for others to follow.

• Those who offered the world new ideas, options, or directions.

Each volume of *World Leaders* begins with a listing of the leaders by country and a timeline showing the chronological relationship among the profiled leaders, the incidents marking their lives, and certain other historical events.

Many sketches in *World Leaders* begin with a short discussion of the social or political environment in which these individuals arose. Where possible, childhood and educational experiences of the chosen leaders have been highlighted. Philosophical or religious ideas or movements that directed the course of the leaders' actions are explained in the text. Some of these ideas or movements, such as Stoicism or the Enlightenment, are given a fuller discussion in sidebars, more than a dozen of which are sprinkled throughout the three volumes. Other sidebars present varied topics—from the U.S. cost in the Vietnam War to a Shaker hymn—that are both informative and interesting.

Each biographical sketch in *World Leaders* contains a portrait of the profiled leader and the date and the place of that person's birth and death, or the dates of his or her reign. To provide readers with a clearer understanding of the geographical descriptions in the text, maps are placed within some sketches. A comprehensive subject index concludes each volume.

Acknowledgments

We wish to extend a humble note of thanks to the U·X·L family: Tom Romig, for graciously handing us this project; Kathleen Witman, for insightfully emending the style of the text; and, finally, Sonia Benson, for gently shepherding the work to its completion.

We welcome any comments on this work and suggestions for future volumes of *World Leaders.* Please write: Editors, *World Leaders,* U·X·L, Gale Research Inc., 835 Penobscot Bldg., Detroit, Michigan 48226-4094; call toll-free: 1-800-877-4253; or fax: 313-961-6348.

World Leaders by Country

A listing of leaders by the central country or countries in which they ruled or made changes. When possible, ancient empires, city-states, and kingdoms have been listed with an asterisk under the modern-day country in which they were once located.

Argentina:

José de San Martín
(1778-1850)

Eva Marie Duarte de Perón
(1919-1952)

Juan Domingo Perón
(1895-1974)

Assyria (ancient empire including vast region of western Asia):
Ashurbanipal
(c. 700-c. 626 B.C.)

Babylon (ancient city-state near present day Baghdad, Iraq):

Hammurabi
(ruled c. 1792-1759 B.C.)

Bolivia:

Simón Bolívar
(1783-1830)

Canada:

Samuel de Champlain
(c. 1570-1635)

Carthage (city-state in present-day Tunisia):
Hannibal
(247-183 B.C.)

China:

Chiang Kai-shek
(1887-1975)
Confucius
(c. 551-c. 479 B.C.)
Lao-tzu
(c. sixth century B.C.)
Mao Zedong
(1893-1976)
Qin Shi Huang-di
(259-210 B.C.)
Zhao Kuang-yin
(927-976)

Colombia:

Simón Bolívar
(1783-1830)

Cuba:

Ernesto "Ché" Guevara
(1928-1967)
José Martí
(1853-1895)

Denmark:

Canute I, the Great
(c. 995-1035)
Margaret I
(1353-1412)

Egypt:

Cleopatra VII
(69-30 B.C.)
Hatshepsut
(c. 1520-c. 1468 B.C.)
Moses
(c. late 13th century–
c. early 11th century B.C.)

Gamal Abdal Nasser
(1918-1970)
Ptolemy I Soter
(367-285 B.C.)
Ramses II
(c. 1315-c. 1225 B.C.)

England:

Alfred the Great
(848-c. 900)
Canute I, the Great
(c. 995-1035)
Winston Churchill
(1874-1965)
Elizabeth I
(1533-1603)
Victoria
(1819-1901)
William the Conqueror
(c. 1027-1087)

Ethiopia:

Haile Selassie I
(1892-1975)

France:

Eleanor of Aquitaine
(1122-1204)
Joan of Arc
(c. 1412-1431)
Louis XIV
(1638-1715)
Napoleon I Bonaparte
(1769-1821)

Germany:

Adolf Hitler
(1889-1945)

Martin Luther
   (1483-1546)
Rudolf I, of Habsburg
   (1218-1291)

Haiti:

Toussaint L'Ouverture
   (1743-1803)

Hungary:

Stephen I
   (c. 973-1038)

India:

Akbar
   (1542-1605)
Mohandas Gandhi
   (1869-1948)
Jawaharlal Nehru
   (1889-1964)
Siddhartha
   (c. 563-c. 483 B.C.)
Mother Teresa
   (1910—)

Iran (formerly Persia):

Abbas I
   (1571-1629)
Cyrus II, the Great
   (c. 590-c. 529)
Ruhollah Khomeini
   (c. 1902-1989)
Zoroaster
   (c. 588-c. 511 B.C.)

Ireland:

Saint Patrick
   (c. 395-c. 460)

Israel:

David Ben-Gurion
   (1886-1973)
King David
   (ruled 1010-970 B.C.)
Jesus of Nazareth
   (c. 6 B.C.-c. A.D. 26)
Moses
   (c. late 13th century–
   c. early 11th century B.C.)

Italy (also see Roman Empire):

Francis of Assisi
   (1182-1226)
John XXIII
   (1881-1963)

Japan:

Fujiwara Michinaga
   (966-1028)

Kenya:

Jomo Kenyatta
   (1891-1978)

Macedonia:

Alexander the Great
   (356-323 B.C.)

Mexico:

Juana Inés de la Cruz
   (1648-1695)
Emiliano Zapata
   (1879-1919)
Tenochtitlán:

Moctezuma II
  (c. 1480-1520)

Mongolia:

Genghis Khan
  (c. 1162-1227)

Norway:

Canute I, the Great
  (c. 995-1035)
Margaret I
  (1353-1412)

North Vietnam:

Ho Chi Minh
  (1890-1969)

Pannonia] (area in present-
  day Hungary and eastern
  Austria):
Attila the Hun
  (c. 370-453)

Prussia (former state of
  Central Europe, including
  parts of present-day
  Germany and Poland):
Frederick II, the Great
  (1712-1786)
Karl Marx
  (1818-1883)

Roman Empire:

Augustus
  (63 B.C.-A.D. 14)
Julius Caesar

(100-44 B.C.)
Charlemagne
  (c. 742-814)
Charles V
  (1500-1558)
Constantine I
  (285-337)
Frederick I (Barbarossa)
  (1123-1190)
Gregory I, the Great
  (c. 540-604)
Marcus Aurelius
  (121-180)
Otto I, the Great
  (912-973)
Rudolf I, of Habsburg
  (1218-1291)

Russia:

Catherine II, the Great
  (1729-1796)
Gorbachev, Mikhail
  (1931—)
Ivan IV, the Terrible
  (1530-1584)
Vladimir Lenin
  (1870-1924)
Alexander Nevsky
  (c. 1220-1263)

Saudi Arabia:

Muhammad (c. 570-632)

Scotland:

Mary, Queen of Scots
  (1542-1587)
Robert I, the Bruce
  (1274-1329)

Senegal:

Léopold Sédar Senghor
(1906—)

Spain:

Ferdinand II
(1452-1516)
Isabella I
(1451-1504)

Sweden:

Gustavus Adolphus
(1594-1632)
Margaret I
(1353-1412)

Syria:

Palmyra:
Zenobia
(ruled 267-272)

Turkey:

Byzantine Empire:
Irene of Athens
(c. 752-803)
Theodora
(c. 500-548)
Ottoman Empire:
Osman I
(1259-1326)
Suleiman
(c. 1494-1566)

United Republic of Tanzania:

Julius K. Nyerere
(1922—)

United States:

Jane Addams
(1860-1935)
Susan B. Anthony
(1820-1906)
William Bradford
(1590-1657)
Chief Joseph
(1840-1905)
Crazy Horse
(1841-1877)
Frederick Douglass
(1818-1895)
W. E. B. Du Bois
(1868-1963)
Benjamin Franklin
(1706-1790)
Ulysses S. Grant
(1822-1885)
Thomas Jefferson
(1743-1826)
John F. Kennedy
(1917-1963)
Martin Luther King, Jr.
(1929-1968)
Mother Ann Lee
(1736-1784)
Robert E. Lee
(1807-1870)
Abraham Lincoln
(1809-1865)
Malcolm X
(1925-1965)
Thurgood Marshall
(1908-1993)
Increase Mather
(1639-1723)
Thomas Paine
(1737-1809)

Eleanor Roosevelt
(1884-1962)
Franklin Roosevelt
(1882-1945)
Sitting Bull
(c. 1830-1890)
John Smith
(c. 1580-1631)
Elizabeth Cady Stanton
(1815-1902)
Tecumseh
(c. 1768-1813)
Sojourner Truth
(c. 1797-1883)
Harriet Tubman
(c. 1820-1913)
Booker T. Washington
(1856-1915)
George Washington
(1732-1799)
Roger Williams
(c. 1603-1683)

Venezuela:

Simón Bolívar
(1783-1830)

WORLD LEADERS

People Who Shaped the World

Egyptian Pyramids

Timeline

3000 B.C.   **1500 B.C.**   **550 B.C.**

1010-970 B.C.

1: David unites
Israel and Judah
in a kingdom
centered at
Jerusalem

c. 1792-1750 B.C.

1: Hammurabi creates empire of Babylonia
and devises his famous law code

c. 2680–1200 B.C. • Ancient Egypt

c. 2680-2526 B.C. • 1: Building of the Great Pyramids near Giza,
Egypt

c. 1490-1470 B.C. • 1: Hatshepsut proclaims herself "king" of
Egypt and rules as pharaoh

c. 1250 B.C. • 1: Ramses II builds colossal temple at Abu Simbel

c. 1200 B.C. • 1: Moses leads the Hebrews out of slavery in Egypt
to the land of Canaan

c. 670-626 B.C.

1: Ashurbanipal
creates a great
library in
Nineveh, the
capital city of the
Assyrian Empire

c. 6th century B.C. • Philosophy and Religion

c. 6th century B.C. • 1: Lao-tzu reportedly writes his moral
philosophy in the *Tao Te Ching*

c. 550-511 B.C. • 1: Zoroaster spreads his new religion
throughout the Persian Empire

c. 528 B.C. • 1: Siddhartha founds new religion of Buddhism in
India

c. 520 B.C. • 1: Confucius begins teaching a new moral
philosophy in China

c. 550 B.C.

1: Cyrus II, the Great
conquers Media and begins
building the Persian Empire

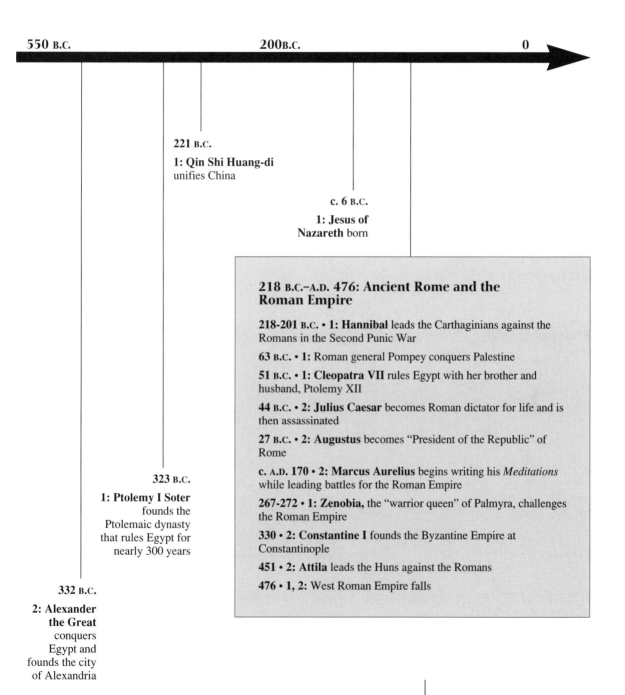

1 = **Volume 1: Asia and Africa**
2 = **Volume 2: Europe**
3 = **Volume 3: North and South America**

550 B.C.   **200B.C.**   **0**

221 B.C.

1: Qin Shi Huang-di
unifies China

c. 6 B.C.

**1: Jesus of
Nazareth** born

**218 B.C.–A.D. 476: Ancient Rome and the
Roman Empire**

218-201 B.C. • 1: Hannibal leads the Carthaginians against the
Romans in the Second Punic War

63 B.C. • 1: Roman general Pompey conquers Palestine

51 B.C. • 1: Cleopatra VII rules Egypt with her brother and
husband, Ptolemy XII

44 B.C. • 2: Julius Caesar becomes Roman dictator for life and is
then assassinated

27 B.C. • 2: Augustus becomes "President of the Republic" of
Rome

c. A.D. 170 • 2: Marcus Aurelius begins writing his *Meditations*
while leading battles for the Roman Empire

267-272 • 1: Zenobia, the "warrior queen" of Palmyra, challenges
the Roman Empire

330 • 2: Constantine I founds the Byzantine Empire at
Constantinople

451 • 2: Attila leads the Huns against the Romans

476 • 1, 2: West Roman Empire falls

323 B.C.

1: Ptolemy I Soter
founds the
Ptolemaic dynasty
that rules Egypt for
nearly 300 years

332 B.C.

**2: Alexander
the Great**
conquers
Egypt and
founds the city
of Alexandria

Charlemagne

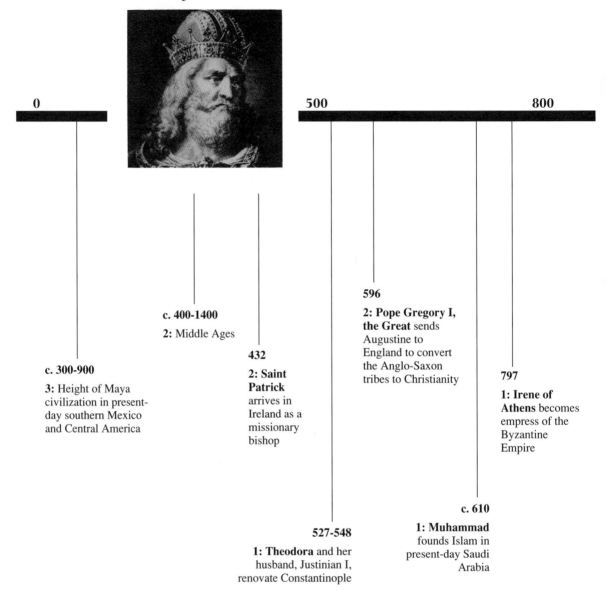

0

500

800

c. 400-1400
2: Middle Ages

c. 300-900

3: Height of Maya
civilization in present-
day southern Mexico
and Central America

432
**2: Saint
Patrick**
arrives in
Ireland as a
missionary
bishop

596
**2: Pope Gregory I,
the Great** sends
Augustine to
England to convert
the Anglo-Saxon
tribes to Christianity

797
**1: Irene of
Athens** becomes
empress of the
Byzantine
Empire

527-548
1: Theodora and her
husband, Justinian I,
renovate Constantinople

c. 610
1: Muhammad
founds Islam in
present-day Saudi
Arabia

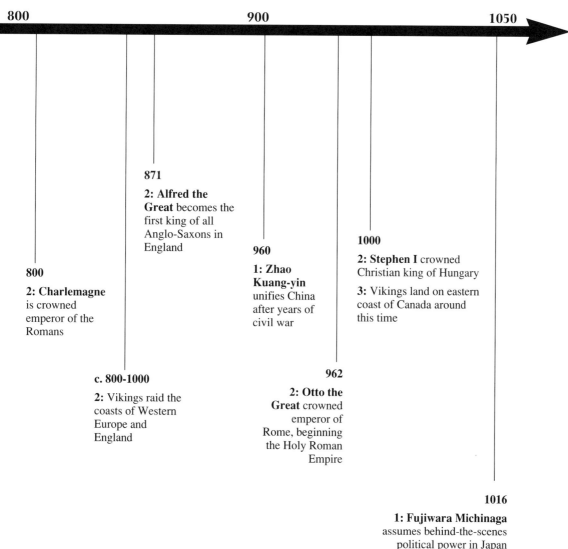

1 = **Volume 1: Asia and Africa**
2 = **Volume 2: Europe**
3 = **Volume 3: North and South America**

800

900

1050

871

2: Alfred the Great becomes the first king of all Anglo-Saxons in England

800

2: Charlemagne is crowned emperor of the Romans

960

1: Zhao Kuang-yin unifies China after years of civil war

1000

2: Stephen I crowned Christian king of Hungary

3: Vikings land on eastern coast of Canada around this time

c. 800-1000

2: Vikings raid the coasts of Western Europe and England

962

2: Otto the Great crowned emperor of Rome, beginning the Holy Roman Empire

1016

1: Fujiwara Michinaga assumes behind-the-scenes political power in Japan

2: Viking **Canute I, the Great** begins rule as king of England, Denmark, and Norway

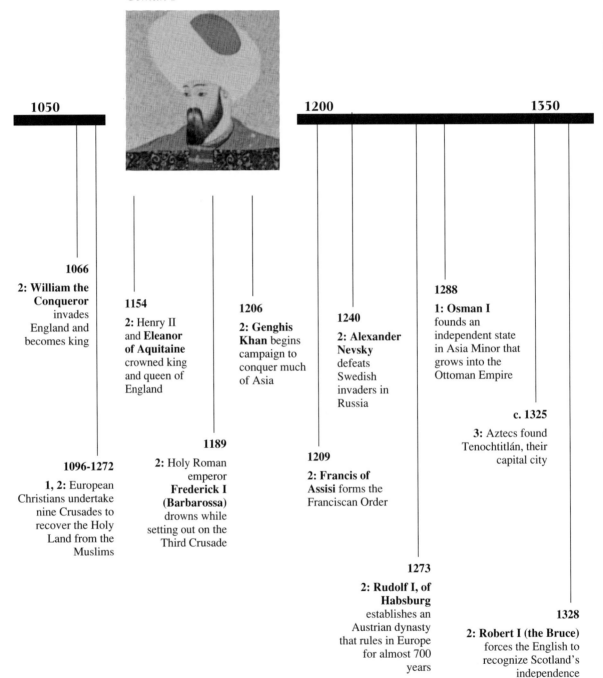

Osman I

1050

1200

1350

1066

2: William the Conqueror invades England and becomes king

1154

2: Henry II and **Eleanor of Aquitaine** crowned king and queen of England

1206

2: Genghis Khan begins campaign to conquer much of Asia

1240

2: Alexander Nevsky defeats Swedish invaders in Russia

1288

1: Osman I founds an independent state in Asia Minor that grows into the Ottoman Empire

c. 1325

3: Aztecs found Tenochtitlán, their capital city

1096-1272

1, 2: European Christians undertake nine Crusades to recover the Holy Land from the Muslims

1189

2: Holy Roman emperor **Frederick I (Barbarossa)** drowns while setting out on the Third Crusade

1209

2: Francis of Assisi forms the Franciscan Order

1273

2: Rudolf I, of Habsburg establishes an Austrian dynasty that rules in Europe for almost 700 years

1328

2: Robert I (the Bruce) forces the English to recognize Scotland's independence

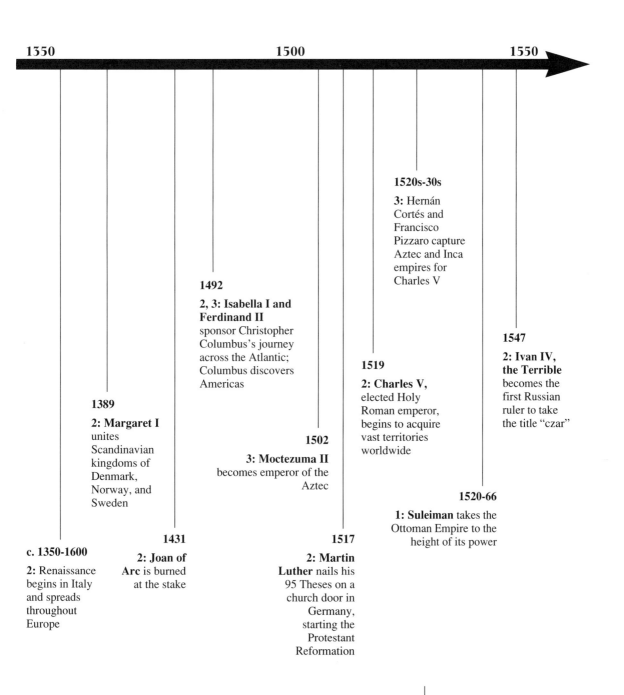

1 = **Volume 1: Asia and Africa**
2 = **Volume 2: Europe**
3 = **Volume 3: North and South America**

1350   **1500**   **1550**

1520s-30s

3: Hernán Cortés and Francisco Pizzaro capture Aztec and Inca empires for Charles V

1492

2, 3: Isabella I and Ferdinand II sponsor Christopher Columbus's journey across the Atlantic; Columbus discovers Americas

1547

2: Ivan IV, the Terrible becomes the first Russian ruler to take the title "czar"

1389

2: Margaret I unites Scandinavian kingdoms of Denmark, Norway, and Sweden

1519

2: Charles V, elected Holy Roman emperor, begins to acquire vast territories worldwide

1502

3: Moctezuma II becomes emperor of the Aztec

1520-66

1: Suleiman takes the Ottoman Empire to the height of its power

c. 1350-1600

2: Renaissance begins in Italy and spreads throughout Europe

1431

2: Joan of Arc is burned at the stake

1517

2: Martin Luther nails his 95 Theses on a church door in Germany, starting the Protestant Reformation

Elizabeth I

1550

1600

1700

1588

2: Elizabeth I's
navy defeats the
Spanish Armada

1611-30

2: Gustavus Adolphus
forms a Swedish empire

1688

**3: Increase
Mather** secures
charter for the
Massachusetts
Bay Colony

1587

1: Abbas I begins rule as
shah of Persia (Iran)

2: Mary, Queen of Scots
is beheaded by the order
of the English queen
Elizabeth I

1654

2: Louis XIV is crowned
king of France

1556

1: Akbar
assumes throne
of the Mughal
Empire in India

1607–1636 • Settlements in North America

1607 • 3: John Smith and others found Jamestown

1608 • 3: Samuel de Champlain founds Quebec

1620 • 3: William Bradford and other Puritans found Plymouth

1636 • 3: Roger Williams founds Providence, Rhode Island

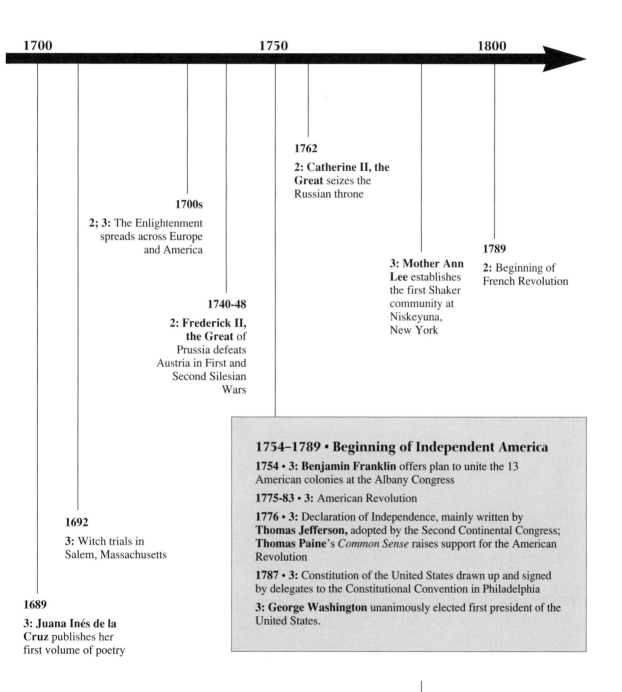

1 = Volume 1: Asia and Africa
2 = Volume 2: Europe
3 = Volume 3: North and South America

1700   1750   1800

1762

2: Catherine II, the Great seizes the Russian throne

1700s

2; 3: The Enlightenment spreads across Europe and America

1789

2: Beginning of French Revolution

3: Mother Ann Lee establishes the first Shaker community at Niskeyuna, New York

1740-48

2: Frederick II, the Great of Prussia defeats Austria in First and Second Silesian Wars

1754–1789 • Beginning of Independent America

1754 • 3: Benjamin Franklin offers plan to unite the 13 American colonies at the Albany Congress

1775-83 • 3: American Revolution

1776 • 3: Declaration of Independence, mainly written by **Thomas Jefferson,** adopted by the Second Continental Congress; **Thomas Paine**'s *Common Sense* raises support for the American Revolution

1787 • 3: Constitution of the United States drawn up and signed by delegates to the Constitutional Convention in Philadelphia

3: George Washington unanimously elected first president of the United States.

1692

3: Witch trials in Salem, Massachusetts

1689

3: Juana Inés de la Cruz publishes her first volume of poetry

Simón Bolívar

1800

1820

1850

1817
3: José de San Martín battles
Spanish forces in Chile

1837-1901
2: Reign of England's
Queen Victoria II

1812
3: Tecumseh and
English forces
capture Detroit

1819
3: Simón Bolívar
proclaimed president
of Greater Colombia

1848
3: Karl Marx and Friedrich Engels
publish the *Communist Manifesto*

1804
**2: Napoleon I
Bonaparte** is
crowned emperor
of France

1831–1870 • Slavery and the American Civil War

1831 • 3: Nat Turner leads a bloody slave uprising in Virginia

1841 • 3: Frederick Douglass gives his first abolitionist speech

1850 • 3: Harriet Tubman leads her first party of slaves to
freedom on the Underground Railroad; **Sojourner Truth**
publishes her autobiography, *Narrative of Sojourner Truth*

1859 • 3: Abolitionist John Brown is hanged after seizing the
government arsenal at Harpers Ferry, Virginia

1861-65 • 3: American Civil War

1862 • 3: Robert E. Lee defeats the Union forces at the Seven
Days' battle and the second battle of Bull Run

1863 • 3: Abraham Lincoln issues the Emancipation
Proclamation; **Ulysses S. Grant** defeats the Confederate forces at
Vicksburg

1865 • 3: Lee surrenders to Grant at Appomattox Courthouse;
Lincoln assassinated by John Wilkes Booth at Ford's Theater

1868 • 3: U.S. Congress adopts the Fourteenth Amendment,
recognizing former slaves as U.S. citizens

1870 • 3: Fifteenth Amendment of U.S. Constitution extends
voting rights to all black males

1812-15
2, 3: War of 1812
between the U.S.
and England

1801

**3: Toussaint
L'Ouverture**
conquers Spanish
colony of Santo
Domingo

Timeline

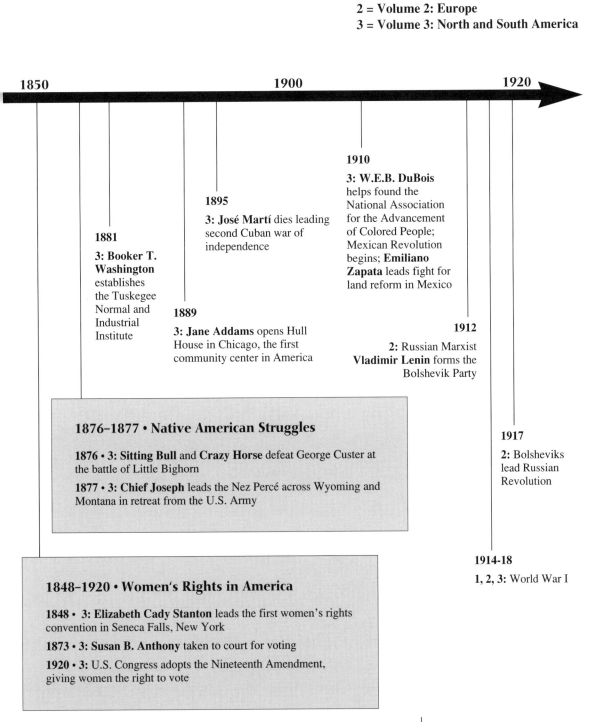

1 = Volume 1: Asia and Africa
2 = Volume 2: Europe
3 = Volume 3: North and South America

1850   1900   1920

1910

3: W.E.B. DuBois helps found the National Association for the Advancement of Colored People; Mexican Revolution begins; **Emiliano Zapata** leads fight for land reform in Mexico

1895

3: José Martí dies leading second Cuban war of independence

1881

3: Booker T. Washington establishes the Tuskegee Normal and Industrial Institute

1889

3: Jane Addams opens Hull House in Chicago, the first community center in America

1912

2: Russian Marxist **Vladimir Lenin** forms the Bolshevik Party

1876–1877 • Native American Struggles

1876 • 3: Sitting Bull and **Crazy Horse** defeat George Custer at the battle of Little Bighorn

1877 • 3: Chief Joseph leads the Nez Percé across Wyoming and Montana in retreat from the U.S. Army

1917

2: Bolsheviks lead Russian Revolution

1914-18

1, 2, 3: World War I

1848–1920 • Women's Rights in America

1848 • 3: Elizabeth Cady Stanton leads the first women's rights convention in Seneca Falls, New York

1873 • 3: Susan B. Anthony taken to court for voting

1920 • 3: U.S. Congress adopts the Nineteenth Amendment, giving women the right to vote

Adolf Hitler

1920

1935

1946

1940

2: Winston Churchill is named prime minister of England

1926

1: Chiang Kai-shek leads his Nationalist army in the Northern Expedition to unify China

1933

2: Adolf Hitler is named chancellor of Germany

3: Franklin D. Roosevelt begins his New Deal program

1939-45

1, 2, 3: World War II

1946

3: Eleanor Roosevelt appointed chairperson of the United Nations Commission on Human Rights

1929

3: Stock-market crash in the U.S. marks the beginning of the Great Depression

1935

1: Haile Selassie I leads his Ethiopian army against the invading Italian forces of Benito Mussolini

1946

3: Juan Domingo Perón elected president of Argentina

1919–1947 • Indian Independence

1919 • 1: Mohandas Gandhi organizes his first nationwide nonviolent demonstration protesting English rule in India

1947 • 1: Jawaharlal Nehru becomes the first prime minister of an independent India

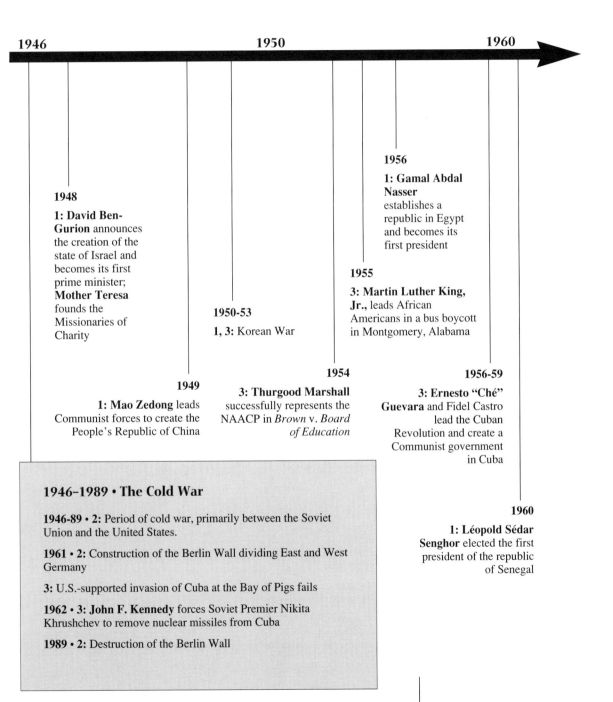

1 = Volume 1: Asia and Africa
2 = Volume 2: Europe
3 = Volume 3: North and South America

1946   1950   1960

1956

1: Gamal Abdal Nasser establishes a republic in Egypt and becomes its first president

1948

1: David Ben-Gurion announces the creation of the state of Israel and becomes its first prime minister; **Mother Teresa** founds the Missionaries of Charity

1955

3: Martin Luther King, Jr., leads African Americans in a bus boycott in Montgomery, Alabama

1950-53

1, 3: Korean War

1949

1: Mao Zedong leads Communist forces to create the People's Republic of China

1954

3: Thurgood Marshall successfully represents the NAACP in *Brown* v. *Board of Education*

1956-59

3: Ernesto "Ché" Guevara and Fidel Castro lead the Cuban Revolution and create a Communist government in Cuba

1960

1: Léopold Sédar Senghor elected the first president of the republic of Senegal

1946–1989 • The Cold War

1946-89 • 2: Period of cold war, primarily between the Soviet Union and the United States.

1961 • 2: Construction of the Berlin Wall dividing East and West Germany

3: U.S.-supported invasion of Cuba at the Bay of Pigs fails

1962 • 3: John F. Kennedy forces Soviet Premier Nikita Khrushchev to remove nuclear missiles from Cuba

1989 • 2: Destruction of the Berlin Wall

John F. Kennedy

1960

1965

1980

1962

2: Pope John XXI opens the Second Vatican Council in Rome

1964

1: Jomo Kenyatta becomes the first president of the newly independent Kenya; **Julius K. Nyerere** unites Tanganyika and Zanzibar to form Tanzania, and becomes its first president

1969

3: U.S. astronaut Neil Armstrong becomes the first person to walk on the moon

1979

1: Ruhollah Khomeini creates an Islamic state in Iran

1963–1968 • Assassinations in America

1963 • 3: John F. Kennedy assassinated in Dallas, Texas

1965 • 3: Malcolm X assassinated in New York

1968 • 3: Martin Luther King, Jr., assassinated in Memphis, Tennessee

1954–1975 • Conflict in Vietnam

1954 • 1: Ho Chi Minh becomes president of Communist North Vietnam after Vietnamese forces defeat the French

1961-73 • 3: U.S. takes part in the Vietnam War

1975 • 1: North Vietnam defeats South Vietnam, uniting the country under a Communist government

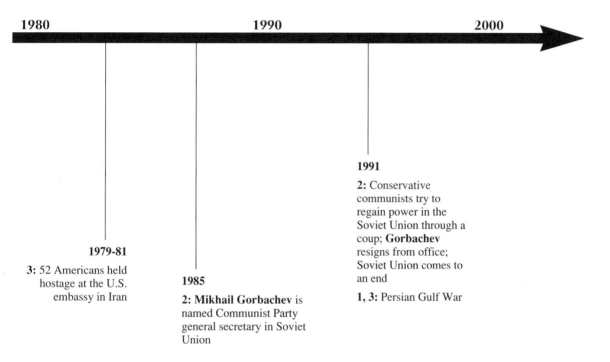

1980   1990   2000

1991

2: Conservative communists try to regain power in the Soviet Union through a coup; **Gorbachev** resigns from office; Soviet Union comes to an end

1, 3: Persian Gulf War

1979-81

3: 52 Americans held hostage at the U.S. embassy in Iran

1985

2: Mikhail Gorbachev is named Communist Party general secretary in Soviet Union

Mikhail Gorbachev

Abbas I

Persian shah
Born January 27, 1571
Died January 19, 1629

When Abbas I came to power in 1587, Persia (present-day Iran) was threatened on the west by the Ottoman Empire and on the northeast by the Uzbeks (from present-day Uzbekistan). Internally, the country was endangered by competing tribal states and poverty. Abbas quickly put an end to this strife and misery. Although ruthless, he transformed Persia from an ancient, underdeveloped country into a modern nation trading with the outside world. He turned his capital, Isfahan, into one of the most celebrated cities in the Muslim world. Under his rule, the people of Persia enjoyed a greater standard of living than at any time between the Middle Ages and modern times.

Abbas was born in 1571, the second son of Shah (Persian king) Muhammad Khudabanda. He was a member of the Safavid dynasty founded in Persia by Shah Ismail in 1499. The assassination of his older brother, Hamza, in 1586 made Abbas heir to the throne. The following year, his father was overthrown and Abbas was named the new shah. Both his broth-

"Although ruthless, Abbas transformed Persia from an ancient, underdeveloped country into a modern nation trading with the outside world."

er's murder and his father's removal were brought about by two rival tribes in Persia. Upon becoming shah, Abbas was determined to put down these rebels.

External threats to Persia drew Abbas's immediate attention. The Ottoman Empire, at war with Persia since 1578, entered into an alliance with Uzbek tribes to attack Persia at the same time. Wisely recognizing he could not defeat the rich and well-organized Ottoman Empire, Abbas signed the Peace of Constantinople in 1590. This treaty gave the empire control of Caucasia, the region between the Black and Caspian seas containing the Caucasus Mountains. Although unfavorable to Persia, the treaty allowed Abbas to concentrate fully on the Uzbeks. He quickly crushed their forces, expelling them from Persia. In 1603 Abbas counterattacked the Ottoman Empire, fighting it periodically for the remainder of his reign. Over time he regained much of the Persian territory lost through the Peace of Constantinople.

Establishes Control of the Persian Military

Abbas's success was largely due to his reorganization of the Persian army. Because the army previously had been a combination of forces from the various tribes in Persia, there was very little unity in it. To strengthen his central government, Abbas abolished the independent tribal states. He reduced the power of the chieftains of the two dominant tribes, the Turkomans and the Qizilbashis. Now in direct control of the government army, Abbas appointed generals who were loyal to him and who obeyed his commands.

Abbas also took action to improve the economic situation of Persia. He developed new roads and bridges, increased industry, and built inns to attract travelers and traders. To broaden the Persian economy, he brought in merchants, craftsmen, and farmers from other areas. Chinese ceramicists helped develop the ceramic industry, which produced tiles and pottery. Sometimes, however, Abbas brought in workers by force. In 1603 he transported much of the population of present-day eastern Armenia into Persia. All of the people from the town of Julfa were forced to move and the town was burned behind them. In

1616 he reportedly seized more than 130,000 men and women from present-day Georgia. Most of the men were drafted into the Persian army while the women were enslaved in harems.

Abbas's economic policies were extremely successful. The recent colonization of America had decreased the Ottoman Empire's trade with Europe. Abbas took advantage of this, founding the southern port of Bandar Abbas on the Strait of Hormuz. Using the Persian Gulf and a route around Africa, he began trading with Dutch, Portuguese, and English merchants. He sold silks and carpets directly to England. Metalwork, textiles, and ceramics were major Persian exports as well.

Builds Isfahan Into a Great Islamic Capital

With the increased wealth brought in by this trade, Abbas was able to move his capital from the small town of Qazvin in northwest Persia to Isfahan near the center of the country. An ancient city on the Zayandarud River, Isfahan had a pleasant climate, fertile soil, and an ample water supply. Abbas called in architects, craftsmen, and artists to decorate his new capital. Lined with trees and canals, Isfahan soon became one of the largest and most beautiful cities in the Islamic world. It grew to be almost 20 miles around, housing one million people. At the center of the city was Maidan-i-Shah, a great rectangular garden. Inside this garden was the royal mosque, Masjid-i-Shah. Other mosques and gardens adorned Isfahan, along with vast bazaars and a royal palace.

Although Abbas had five sons, his own cruelty ensured that none of them succeeded him to the throne. Fearing that he might be overthrown like his father, Abbas neglected his sons, leaving them to be raised in the royal harem. As a result, none of them received the proper training to become a ruler. His second and fourth sons died young. Safi Mirza, his eldest son, was well liked by the Persian people. However, Abbas suspected him of plotting to take the throne and had him executed when he was 27. For unknown reasons, Abbas then blinded his two remaining sons. In 1629, on his deathbed, he chose his grandson, Sam Mirza, to become the new shah. Abbas's practice of not training a new ruler was followed by his successors, leading to the eventual decline of Persia.

Akbar

Great ruler of Mughal Empire
Born 1542,
Umarkot, present-day Pakistan
Died 1605,
Agra, present-day India

"Akbar stands out among historic world leaders for his respect for differing religions, cultures, and ethnic groups."

The Mughal (Mongol) Empire was founded in 1526 when Babar, a direct descendent of the Mongol leader Genghis Khan (see **Genghis Khan**), swept down from central Asia, conquering northern India and establishing the new empire there. However, Babar's claim to this empire was a military one, and his weak son, Humayun, soon lost it. Babar's grandson, Akbar, then regained the Mughal empire and went on to become its greatest ruler. He not only increased the size of the empire but stabilized its government to make it last. Instead of separating the various peoples under his rule, he worked to combine all of them into a unified society. Akbar stands out among historic world leaders for his respect for differing religions, cultures, and ethnic groups.

Akbar was born in 1542 in present-day Pakistan after his father, Humayun, had been driven from the throne in India. While Humayun spent the next thirteen years preparing to recapture the Mughal Empire, Akbar received a prince's proper education. He was trained in horsemanship, hunting, weaponry, and military sciences. Although he never learned to read or to write, he developed a lifelong fondness for being read to and for intellectual discussion. However, he learned early on that a great ruler needed to be a wise judge of men rather than a scholar.

Humayun invaded India in 1555 and reestablished the Mughal Empire, but died the following year. Only 14 at the time, Akbar assumed the throne with Bayram Khan, his regent (person who ruled in his place until he came of age). In 1560 Akbar launched a 15-year span of conquest. The greatest threat to Akbar and his Muslim rule in India came from the Rajputs, people who controlled regions in northwestern India. The Rajputs were followers of Hinduism, a religion directly opposed to Islam, the religion of the Muslims. Whereas Islam was monotheistic (belief in only one god), Hinduism was polytheistic (belief in many gods).

Hinduism

Hinduism is one of the oldest religions still practiced in the world. Almost all present-day Hindus live in India. It is believed that Hinduism arose in India as a combination of other religions around 1500 B.C. Due to its complex set of beliefs, Hinduism is difficult to define simply. Traditional features of the religion included a belief that a person's soul kept coming back, either in another person, or in an animal, or in something inanimate like a rock. A person's *karma,* a record of how well they behaved in life, determined in what form they would return in their following life.

Treats All Subjects Equally

Akbar was an excellent general. He directed the course of battles and actually took an active role in the fighting. During his 15-year campaign, Akbar conquered 15 provinces and enlarged the Mughal Empire to cover northern India and the present-day countries of Pakistan and Afghanistan. Akbar was not only a conqueror but an insightful ruler. In order to govern effectively, he needed the loyalty of all people under his control. To achieve this, he appointed Rajput chiefs and members of other conquered groups to high positions in the military and the government. So everyone would be treated equally in the empire, Akbar repealed two taxes: one that had been placed on all non-Muslims and one that had been placed on Hindu pilgrims traveling to holy places. He also accepted Rajput princesses into his harem, eventually marrying one of them.

Having unified the Mughal Empire, Akbar then began to build on it. Humayun had constructed a strong fortress at Agra in northern India and Akbar rebuilt it. He strengthened and enlarged the walls, covering them in red sandstone. Reportedly, the new fort had one hundred gates that opened upon massive administrative buildings, armories, and stables. Even grander than this fort was the city Akbar built in 1569 on a hill south of Agra—Fatehpur Sikri, the new capital of his empire. Huge elephant statues stood by the city's grand gateway, the Buland Darwaza. The buildings inside included a mosque, a mausoleum, a royal hall, and two palaces. Many of these structures were built out of red sandstone; almost all were covered with murals and carvings.

Develops a New Religion

Akbar's interest in art and architecture was exceeded only by his interest in religion. He had become disappointed in Islam and looked to other religions in search of basic truths. He studied Hinduism, Zoroastrianism (see **Zoroaster**), and Christianity. In 1575 he had the Ibadat Khana ("House of Religious Discourse") built at Fatehpur Sikri. Here, learned men of all religions discussed theology with Akbar. In 1582, partly to unify the many people under his rule, Akbar introduced a new religious faith, the *Din-i-Ilahi* ("divine faith"). It combined elements from Islam, Hinduism, Zoroastrianism, and Christianity. Akbar firmly believed he was not only a political leader for his people but a spiritual guide as well.

Although the Mughal Empire was secure and its economy prosperous, Akbar's final years were unhappy. His advisors, many of them his friends, retired or died. His oldest son and successor, Jahangir, was rebellious. He reportedly plotted the murder of Akbar's closest advisor and supporter, Abul Fazl, in 1602. When Akbar died three years later from poisoning, many people at the time considered Jahangir responsible. It was a sad end for the emperor who had ruled with respect and understanding, but his Mughal Empire continued to thrive under his descendants.

Ashurbanipal

Scholar-king of Assyria
Born c. 700 B.C.
Died c. 626 B.C.

The empire of Assyria reached its height under the rule of Ashurbanipal. This empire—the largest the world had ever seen—controlled a vast region in western Asia. In modern times, this area would include all or portions of the countries of Iran, Kuwait, Iraq, Turkey, Syria, Lebanon, Jordan, Israel, and Saudi Arabia. The Assyrians were savage warriors. Once they defeated an enemy, they looted all the treasures and resources of the conquered country. Then they set up an ordered government and a taxation system to maintain control over that country. With the riches he drew in, Ashurbanipal made the Assyrian capital of Nineveh into a magnificent city. The constant revolts against Assyrian rule, however, brought an end to this city and the empire soon after his death.

Ashurbanipal was born around 700 B.C. to the Assyrian king Esar-Haddon. As the future king, Ashurbanipal was expected to be wise and powerful. Growing up, he received both academic and military training. His father was continually engaged in battles not only to maintain the empire but also

"Ashurbanipal's reign was one of the greatest in Assyrian history but was also one of its last."

to extend it. Around 673 B.C., Esar-Haddon began a three-year conquest of Egypt. Even though he was victorious in battle, he failed to capture the Egyptian king Taharqa. When Esar-Haddon left Egypt, Taharqa regained control of his country.

Esar-Haddon died before he could respond to Taharqa. Assuming his father's throne, Ashurbanipal led an army back to Egypt and quickly recaptured it. A few rebellions erupted soon after the Assyrians set up a government, but the army quickly crushed them. Impressed by Necho, one of the rebel leaders, Ashurbanipal placed him in command of the government. This diplomatic and forgiving move soon proved to be Ashurbanipal's undoing in Egypt.

Constantly Battles Rebellions

Over the next several years, Ashurbanipal had to contend with attacks by the kingdom of Elam, located in the region of present-day southwestern Iran. For a very long time, there had been peace between Elam and Assyria. During Ashurbanipal's battles in Egypt, however, the Elamites invaded Assyrian territory. Sending troops to the area, Ashurbanipal eventually regained control of his lands. He then conquered Elam, placing a king of his own choosing on the Elamite throne. But while Ashurbanipal was engaged in these campaigns, Necho's son, Psamtik, led another revolt in Egypt that successfully expelled the Assyrians. They never returned to regain control of Egypt.

The greatest threat to Ashurbanipal's rule came from his brother Shamash-shum-ukin. Esar-Haddon had given him control of Babylonia, a country in the area between present-day Baghdad, Iraq, and the Persian Gulf. After remaining loyal to his brother for more than 15 years, Shamash-shum-ukin rose in revolt. He tried to draw support from other leaders under Assyrian control but was unsuccessful. The brothers fought for almost five years. Finally, Ashurbanipal seized control of the capital city of Babylon, killing many of it inhabitants. Not wanting to be captured, Shamash-shum-ukin committed suicide by setting his palace on fire. Afterward, Ashurbanipal placed Babylonia under his domain.

Struggles for the throne in Elam soon drew Ashurbanipal back to that country. Furious at the almost constant rebellions and betrayals of the Elamite kings, Ashurbanipal had his army ravage the country and sack the capital city of Susa. He then returned to Assyria with an enormous quantity of treasure gathered from the campaign. Almost completely destroyed, Elam became a province of the Assyrian Empire.

Both the yearly tributes (taxes) paid by conquered countries and the booty taken during battles made the empire wealthy. Ashurbanipal increased the splendor of Nineveh, located near the present-day city of Mosul, Iraq. He built a magnificent royal palace of sun-dried clay bricks adorned with brilliantly colored enameled tiles. The bas-reliefs (sculpted pictures) of lions and other animals that decorated the walls are considered masterpieces of Assyrian art.

Builds Great Library at Nineveh

The most important of Ashurbanipal's buildings, however, was the library he had built in the palace complex. (This library was discovered almost intact by archaeologists in the 1840s). Proud of his learning, Ashurbanipal ordered his scribes to copy ancient books from countries throughout the empire. Over 20,000 clay tablets were found in this library. Written in cuneiform (wedge-shaped characters used to represent words or ideas), the tablets contain historical, political, religious, and literary works. The large number of scientific texts found there contain information on such areas as mathematics, botany, zoology, chemistry, and astronomy. Most modern knowledge about Assyrian history and culture comes from these tablets.

Ashurbanipal's reign was one of the greatest in Assyrian history but was also one of its last. His brutality made him no new allies and cost him the ones he had. When he died around 626 B.C., the empire was in decline. Less than fifteen years later, the governor of Babylon joined with others to seize Nineveh. They destroyed the city and, with it, the Assyrian Empire.

David Ben-Gurion

One of the founders of the state of Israel

Born October 16, 1886,
Plonsk, Poland

Died December 1, 1973,
Israel

"It was Ben-Gurion's voice that announced to the rest of the world in 1948 the creation of the state of Israel."

When David Ben-Gurion was a young boy growing up in present-day Poland in the late 1800s, he listened to his grandfather's many tales of Jewish history. Afterward, he would sit dreaming of *Eretz Israel* (Hebrew for "Land of Israel"). At this same time, other Jews in Europe also dreamed of the creation of a Jewish nation state, and a movement to achieve this, called Zionism, soon spread. According to Jewish tradition, God promised the land of Palestine to the Jews. An ancient region on the eastern shore of the Mediterranean Sea, Palestine occupied lands that form parts of present-day Israel, Jordan, and Egypt. This is where the Jews wanted to establish their homeland, and Ben-Gurion spent much of his life fighting for this dream. It was his voice that announced to the rest of the world in 1948 the creation of the state of Israel.

The French Revolution (begun in 1789) had given rise to the idea that a people and their nation were inseparable. This in turn had fostered nationalism, the belief that one's culture or nation was superior to all others, and it spread over Europe in the nineteenth century. At this time Jews, who did not have their own country but lived throughout Europe, were experiencing prejudice against them, called anti-Semitism. Theodor Herzl, a Hungarian Jewish journalist, believed the only way to combat anti-Semitism was to create a Jewish nation. In 1896 he published his views in a pamphlet, *Der Judenstaat* ("The Jewish State"), and Zionism was born.

Ben-Gurion had been born David Grün ten years earlier in the Polish village of Plonsk, then under control of the Russians. Filled with his grandfather's tales and the growing idea of Zionism, Grün traveled to Palestine in 1906. Along with other Jewish settlers, he cleared rocks and swamps for farmland in Galilee, a region in northern Palestine. In 1910 he traveled south to the city of Jerusalem to work as a journalist. Here he adopted the name of Ben-Gurion in honor of a Hebrew defender of Jerusalem who died fighting the Romans in A.D. 70.

The Turkish Ottoman Empire had been in control of Palestine since 1516. When World War I began in 1914, the empire allied itself with Germany, and many Jews fled from Palestine. Ben-Gurion, however, decided to remain to organize more settlements and a general Jewish militia. In response, the Turkish officials expelled him from Palestine in 1915, and Ben-Gurion sailed to New York City. Once in the United States, he started a movement to encourage young American Jews to work as pioneers in Palestine. In 1917 he married Paula Munweiss, an American nurse.

Unites Jewish Factions in Palestine

During the war, England had gained control of Palestine. In 1917 the English government issued the Balfour Declaration, stating England's support for the creation of a Jewish state in Palestine. Ben-Gurion traveled back to Palestine the following year and, during the 1920s, worked to organize Jewish pioneers, workers, and farmers. In 1930 he successfully united the various political groups in Palestine by forming the Mapai (Workers' United) party under his leadership. It became the most powerful political force in Palestine. Three years later Ben-Gurion was named chair of the Jewish Agency Executive, which had been created by the League of Nations to act as a Jewish governing body in Palestine.

In the mid-1930s, Jews poured into Palestine, fleeing Nazism in Europe (see **Adolf Hitler**). Muslim Arabs in the area soon revolted against the tremendous increase of Jewish settlers. These Arabs also wanted to settle Palestine for religious reasons. According to Islamic teachings, the prophet Muhammad (see **Muhammad**) ascended into heaven from Jerusalem. Tensions between Jews and Arabs soon turned violent. In 1939 the English government issued an order that set a limit on the number of Jews entering Palestine. Ben-Gurion and his fellow Jewish leaders strongly opposed the order, but when World War II started that same year, they supported England and its allies against Germany.

The end of World War II in 1945 brought to light the horrific event of the Holocaust—the murder of six million European Jews by Hitler and the Nazis. This did little to change England's policy preventing more Jewish immigrants from entering Palestine. In response, Ben-Gurion organized the smuggling of Jews into the area. Fearing the situation could no longer be managed, England handed control of Palestine over to the United Nations in 1947. The UN set up a plan to divide Palestine between the Jews and the Arabs, but the Arabs rejected the plan, demanding all of Palestine. Both sides then prepared for war.

Declares the Existence of Israel

On May 14, 1948, Ben-Gurion went on the radio in the city of Tel Aviv to announce the creation of the state of Israel. He immediately became prime minister and defense minister of the new Jewish state. The following day, the Arab armies of Egypt, Syria, Jordan, and Lebanon attacked Israel. Ben-Gurion then united all the Jewish fighting forces that had existed in Palestine into a single Israeli army. Over the next year, the Israelis pushed the Arab forces out of Israel, even gaining more territory in the process. In 1949 the Arab states signed a treaty recognizing the new borders of Israel.

Ben-Gurion held his government positions until 1953, and then again from 1955 through 1963. Even though a treaty had been signed between Israel and its Arab neighbors, tensions continued to grow in the area. In 1955 Egypt seized the Suez Canal (waterway connecting the Mediterranean Sea with the Red Sea), which had been controlled by France and England. It then attacked Israeli borders. Ben-Gurion ordered a counterattack. Along with French and English forces, the Israeli army reopened the canal and stopped the Egyptian attacks.

In his first ten years as prime minister, Ben-Gurion helped bring more than one million Jews to Israel. Because of controversy over possible spying by his government, he resigned as prime minister in 1963. Two years later, he broke with the Mapai party and formed a new party called Rafi. He was elected to the Knesset, the Israeli legislature, that year and again in 1969. However, his once-great political influence was over by then. Ben-Gurion died of a cerebral hemorrhage on December 1, 1973.

Chiang Kai-shek

Chinese Nationalist leader

*Born October 30, 1887,
Chikow, Chekiang*

*Died April 5, 1975,
Taiwan*

"As a soldier and a politician, Chiang was the controlling force in Chinese politics for 20 years."

When he was 18 years old, Chiang Kai-shek decided to become a soldier and traveled to Tokyo, Japan, which had the best military academies in Asia. While there, he became involved with Chinese revolutionaries who wanted to overthrow the Manchus, a minority ethnic group from the northeast province of Manchuria. The Manchus had held control of China's government since 1644. Chiang and the other revolutionaries wanted to form a Nationalist government that would strengthen China and represent the majority of its people. They were successful, and Chiang became the leader of the ruling party. As a soldier and a politician, he was the controlling force in Chinese politics for 20 years. A growing Communist movement in China, however, soon toppled his Nationalist government, and a new era began in China's history.

Chiang was born in 1887 in the tiny village of Chikow in the east coast province of Chekiang. His father, Chiang Su-an, was a moderately successful salt merchant who died when Chiang was eight. Raised by his mother, Wang Tsai-yu, and his grandfather, Chiang spent the remainder of his childhood in poverty. After traveling to Tokyo in 1905, he met the Chinese revolutionary leader Sun Yat-sen. His growing revolutionary activities, however, prevented Chiang from gaining entrance into a Japanese academy, and he was forced to attend a Chinese academy instead. He was finally admitted to a military academy in Tokyo in 1907. After graduating in 1909, he served two years in the Japanese army.

Chiang returned to China in 1911 after learning that a revolution against the Manchus had begun. After the collapse of the Manchus in 1912, Sun Yat-sen formed a government, with Yüan Shikai serving as its president. When Yüan died in 1916, chaos reigned in China. Power in the country fell into the hands of some 200 military generals, or warlords, who controlled numerous regions. In 1918 Sun Yat-sen established a new government in Guangzhou (in southeast China) with Chiang as his personal military advisor. The majority of the warlords supported a rival government that had been set up in Beijing (in northeast China).

Seeking support for Sun's revolutionary government, Chiang traveled to the Soviet Union in 1923 to study its military and social systems. After he returned, he became commandant of a new military academy at Whampoa, ten miles outside of Guangzhou. Although the academy was set up following a Soviet model, Chiang refused to embrace communism.

Leads Northern Expedition to Unify China

When Sun died in 1925, Chiang became leader of the Kuomintang, the ruling party of the government. At this time, the Kuomintang controlled only two southern regions. Eager to defeat the powerful warlords and unify the country, Chiang began a military campaign called the Northern Expedition in 1926. His Nationalist army defeated many warlord armies, absorbing them into its own ranks. Within a year, the wealthy provinces of southern, central, and eastern China were under Nationalist control. On March 24, 1927, Chiang seized the eastern city of Nanjing, which he then proclaimed as China's new capital.

Under Sun, the Kuomintang had cooperated with the growing Communist movement in China, but Chiang reversed that policy. He ordered the execution of thousands of Communists and forced those in the Kuomintang to resign. By 1928 the Kuomintang was decidedly anti-Communist. Chiang then launched the second stage of the Northern Expedition. After capturing the warlord capital of Beijing in June of 1928, his massive military campaign came to an end. He became the unquestioned leader of the majority of China for the next 20 years.

Chiang then began modernizing China. Hospitals, high schools, universities, airports, and power stations were built throughout the country. Telephone lines were installed in remote regions and 75,000 miles of road were laid. He balanced China's budget and stabilized its currency. Although the cities prospered, farming areas remained poor. Most crops were still harvested by hand. Lacking proper medical care, many farm children died.

In 1931 Japan seized Manchuria, but Chiang decided not to regain the region. He felt it necessary first to attack China's growing Communist movement, which had proclaimed a Chinese Soviet Republic in the southwest region of the country. Although the fighting was fierce and thousands of Communists were killed, Chiang could not effectively crush the movement. The Communists appealed to Chiang to stop the civil war and to turn against the Japanese, but he refused. In December of 1936, while in the province of Xi'an, Chiang was kidnapped by the warlord Zhang Xueliang. Sympathetic to the Communists, Zhang refused to release Chiang until he agreed to halt all attacks against the Communists. Chiang agreed to a truce.

Chinese and Japanese Battle on the Marco Polo Bridge

On July 7, 1937, Chinese troops clashed with a Japanese force at the Marco Polo Bridge near Beijing, and full-scale war broke out. Whatever chance Chiang had of establishing a strong central government was gone. By the fall of 1938, he had lost all of eastern China. A million Japanese occupied eight provinces, including every harbor along the coastline. Because the Japanese controlled the most fertile farmland in the country, Chiang's Nationalist government seized the food of the poorer peasants, leaving five million Chinese to starve.

In 1941 the war in China became part of World War II. The United States and England sent needed supplies to Chiang to help in his effort against Japan. Even with the additional aid, Chiang was not able to defeat the Japanese until the late summer of 1945. The end of the war, however, did not bring peace to China. What little cooperation there had been between the Nationalists and the Communists during the war soon dissolved. Civil war broke out again in 1946. The long war with Japan had weakened the Nationalist government and the Communists, under the leadership of Mao Zedong (see **Mao Zedong**), made steady gains. By the end of 1947, they controlled most of Manchuria. By the end of 1948, they controlled the northern provinces.

Unable to stop the Communists in the south, Chiang and his government were forced to flee on December 10, 1949, to the island of Taiwan, 100 miles off the east coast of China. Here he set up his Nationalist government. Even though he ruled as a virtual dictator, the Taiwanese economy prospered under his control. Chiang promised to retake China from the Communists, but never did. In 1972 the United Nations recognized the Communist Party as the legal government of China, rejecting Taiwan's previous claim. Chiang died of a heart attack in Taiwan three years later.

Cleopatra VII

Queen of Egypt
Born 69 B.C.,
Egypt
Died 30 B.C.,
Egypt

"The ambitious Cleopatra dreamed of ruling a vast empire from Alexandria."

Cleopatra VII is one of the most famous of the Ptolemaic rulers who governed Egypt for over 300 years, beginning with Ptolemy I Soter (see **Ptolemy I Soter**). Under the Ptolemies, the Egyptian capital of Alexandria became a center of Hellenism, the ideas and culture of ancient Greece. It also became a leading city of trade in the Mediterranean region, bringing much wealth to Egypt. With the rise of Rome, however, the power of Egypt fell. When Cleopatra came to the throne, fueled by great intelligence and ambition, she sought to restore Egyptian might and independence. Though it ended tragically, her life has come down through history as a romantic legend.

Cleopatra was born in 69 B.C. to Ptolemy XI and his sister Cleopatra Tryphaina (it was Egyptian custom for rulers to marry their siblings). Recognizing her intelligence early, Ptolemy XI made sure she received a wide education. Cleopatra was taught to speak many languages, including Egyptian (the only Ptolemy ever to do so). She also was tutored in governmental affairs.

Rome Seeks to Control Egypt

The power of Rome was spreading over the Mediterranean at this time. Ptolemy XI knew Rome wanted to make Egypt one of its provinces. He also knew Egypt could not oppose the might of the Roman military. To keep Egypt independent, he began to bribe influential Roman senators. Over the centuries, the Ptolemies had acquired a great royal treasury by funneling money away from the Egyptian economy. Ptolemy XI's lavish spending on key senators kept Egypt free from Roman rule, but turned the Egyptian people against him.

Before his death in 51 B.C., Ptolemy XI married Cleopatra to her younger brother Ptolemy XII so they would rule together. However, neither of them wanted to share the throne and they plotted against each other. In 48 B.C. a group of Ptolemy XII's guardians removed Cleopatra from Alexandria. That same year, Julius Caesar (see **Julius Caesar**) and Pompey, the consul (manager) of Rome, battled over the control of Rome. Caesar chased Pompey to Egypt, where Pompey was soon murdered.

Cleopatra knew Caesar wielded great power. Seeking his aid in her struggle, she rolled herself up in a rug and had it smuggled into his quarters in Alexandria. He quickly became enchanted with her and agreed to lend his help. In 47 B.C., in what came to be known as the Alexandrian War, Caesar and Cleopatra battled Ptolemy XII and his guardians. Ptolemy XII soon drowned during a battle on the Nile River. Caesar then placed Cleopatra and her 12-year-old brother on the Egyptian throne. Although Cleopatra and Ptolemy XIII were married, she continued her relationship with Caesar. After bearing him a son, Ptolemy Caesarion, she returned with Caesar to Rome.

Seduces Marc Antony

After Caesar's assassination in 44 B.C., Cleopatra fled back to Egypt to maintain her control there. She had Ptolemy XIII murdered, then proclaimed joint rule with her infant son, now known as Ptolemy XIV Caesarion. Marc Antony, a friend of Caesar, had become one of the leaders of Rome after Caesar's death. He demanded a meeting with Cleopatra, but she refused his requests. Finally, in 41 B.C., she decided to meet Antony at Tarsus (ancient city in present-day southern Turkey). Dressed as Venus, the Roman goddess of love and beauty, Cleopatra traveled to Tarsus on a perfumed barge with purple sails and silver oars. Her plan was to enchant Antony so she would have a powerful ally in Rome and would retain control over Egypt. It worked.

Although Cleopatra bore Antony twin sons in 40 B.C., he returned to Rome to settle a dispute with his co-rulers, Lepidus and Octavian (later known as Augustus—see **Augustus**). The three divided up the Roman world. Antony received control of Rome's eastern regions and married Octavian's sister, Octavia. The allure of Cleopatra, however, was too much for Antony. He returned to her in 37 B.C.

The ambitious Cleopatra dreamed of ruling a vast empire from Alexandria. After she married Antony in 36 B.C., he gave her large territories that had previously been part of Roman domain. When this news reached Rome, Octavian stripped Antony of his powers and the Roman Senate declared Antony an enemy of the state. Soon after, the Senate declared war on Antony and Cleopatra. In 31 B.C. Octavian defeated the forces of Antony and Cleopatra in a great sea battle near the ancient town of Actium on the western shore of Greece. While defending Alexandria against an invasion by Octavian in 30 B.C., Antony received a false report that Cleopatra had been killed. He immediately left the battlefield and fell on his sword. A few days later, Octavian captured Cleopatra. While being held prisoner in her chamber, Cleopatra committed suicide by letting an asp (a poisonous snake) bite her. Her death marked the end of the Ptolemaic dynasty and of Egypt's freedom from Roman control.

Confucius

Chinese philosopher and teacher
Born c. 551 B.C.
Lu, present-day Shandong, China
Died c. 479 B.C.
Lu

From about 1025 B.C. to 250 B.C. China was ruled by kings of the Chou dynasty. Because of the country's vast size, these kings had difficulty controlling all areas. Large regions remained under the control of local princes. By 800 B.C. these princes had gained enough power to begin battling not only the Chou kings but each other for control of lands. Disorder reigned in the kingdom. Yet the latter part of the Chou dynasty is known as the classical age of China. Philosophers and other wise men sought new ways to solve the political problems in the country. Among this group was the philosopher Confucius. He offered a philosophy, which came to be known as Confucianism, calling for moral responsibility on the part of both rulers and subjects. Confucianism became the official philosophy of China and greatly influenced its culture for almost 2,000 years.

Confucius was born around 551 B.C. in the state of Lu (present-day province of Shandong). His real name was K'ung Ch'ui. Confucius is the western spelling of K'ung Fu-tzu

"Confucianism became the official philosophy of China and greatly influenced its culture for almost 2,000 years."

(meaning Master K'ung). His father, Shuliang-He, was part of the lesser nobility in Lu, but died before Confucius was three years old. His mother, Yan-Zhenzai, raised him alone. The family soon fell into poverty, and Confucius was forced to work at various jobs while growing up. As a result, he received what education he could on his own.

Tries to Change Leaders' Views

The hardship of his early years gave Confucius an understanding of the sufferings of the common people around him. He saw that the petty battles between princes contributed to the famine and poverty sweeping across the land. To Confucius, the princes appeared more interested in their own personal gain than in the welfare of the people they ruled. He believed it was his mission to convince these rulers to change their ways.

Confucius married Qiguan-shi in 532 B.C., then set about developing a philosophy to restore political harmony. He studied ancient Chinese culture and sought to reinterpret its traditions to provide a new approach to managing society. He hoped to secure a high position in government so he could put into practice his ideas for reform. By the time he was 30, however, his political career had faltered and he decided to begin teaching his ideas to others.

Confucius believed the problems in society stemmed from the poor attitudes of those who ruled. He sought to train a group of civil servants who would have principles. A future leader did not have to be an expert administrator, only a humane and honest individual. Believing anyone could become a person of principles, Confucius wanted to set up as many primary schools as possible throughout China. In this way, even talented poor children could enter government service.

Develops Concepts of *Li* and *Jen*

Confucius's teachings focused on the traditional Chinese concept of *li*. This term stood for proper etiquette or social ritual. At the time, most people interpreted *li* as the proper conduct of ceremonies or rituals. Confucius extended the idea of *li* to govern all people's relationships and behavior. He believed harmony in society would be maintained if people followed this moral etiquette.

Respect was a key element in Confucius's concept of *li*. It governed five principle relationships: those between ruler and subject, parent and child, husband and wife, eldest son and younger brothers, and elders and juniors. Confucius believed respect in these relationships was important for society to function properly.

For Confucius, *li* was the proper way for people to act among other people. He then developed the concept of *jen* to govern the way people acted as individuals. Sometimes *jen* simply meant to love others. More often, it meant humanity, or the quality or state of being human. To improve one's humanity, a person lived by all the moral virtues—wisdom, courage, honor, kindness, and love.

According to Confucius, the combination of *li* and *jen* produced a mature person. To describe this person, Confucius used the traditional term *chun-tzu,* meaning gentleman or aristocrat. The *chun-tzu* was a person of total moral virtue. Confucius thought that kings and leaders who were *chun-tzu* would put the welfare of their subjects first and would rule by moral example.

Confucius attracted many followers, including some in high government positions. His ideas, however, did little to bring about change in his own day. After having taught for many years, he journeyed through various states seeking a government office. These travels were dangerous and Confucius found no ruler willing to give him an important post. Finally, he returned to Lu and continued his teaching until he died at the age of 72. Afterward, his disciples collected his lectures and sayings into a book, the *Analects.* Over the next few centuries, Confucianism spread to become an essential part of Chinese society.

Cyrus II, the Great

Founder of the Persian Empire
Born c. 590 B.C.
Died c. 529 B.C.

"When Cyrus arrived, the Babylonians greeted him not as a conqueror but as a liberator, spreading green branches on the ground before him."

Persia is the ancient name for the modern country of Iran. In the sixth century B.C., Cyrus II turned this kingdom into an empire that lasted for centuries until conquered by the Macedonian king Alexander the Great (see **Alexander the Great**). Cyrus created the Persian Empire by overpowering the countries of Media (present-day western Iran), Lydia (present-day northwestern Turkey), and Babylonia (area between present-day Baghdad, Iraq, and the Persian Gulf). Unlike other soldier-kings, he ruled justly over his conquered lands. Because he allowed many people to return to their homelands and to worship their own gods, Cyrus became known as "the Great."

Hardly any factual information exists about Cyrus's early years, and many historians cannot agree on who his parents were. Herodotus, a Greek historian from the fifth century B.C., wrote that Cyrus was the son of Cambyses I, a Persian noble, and Mandane, the daughter of the Median king Astyages. Many legends, some fantastic, surround the childhood of

Cyrus. One states that he grew up in the mountains of Persia, was nursed by a female dog, and then raised by a shepherd.

Begins Building an Empire

It is known that Cyrus began ruling over the Persian region of Anshan around 559 B.C. Sometime over the next ten years, he secured his position over the other areas in Persia. He then started his quest to build the Persian Empire by attacking Media. After a three-year struggle, he defeated and captured Astyages. On the site of the key battle, he founded his new capital city, Pasargadae (in present-day southwestern Iran). After his victory, Cyrus marched to Ecbatana, the Median capital, and carried its treasures back to his own capital.

In the mid-sixth century B.C., Lydia was the most important kingdom in Asia Minor (peninsula forming most of present-day Turkey). The Lydian king Croesus ruled from the splendid capital city of Sardis near the Mediterranean Sea. Seeking to conquer this area, Cyrus attacked in 547 B.C. According to Herodotus, the first battle between Cyrus and Croesus took place in November and was indecisive. Croesus returned to Sardis and asked his three powerful allies—Sparta, Egypt, and Mesopotamia—to help him in his fight the following spring. Cyrus, however, attacked Sardis that winter and the city quickly fell. Cyrus also gained control of the Greek cities along the west coast of Asia Minor that had been under Lydian rule.

By 540 B.C. the western portion of the Persian Empire was secure. Cyrus then turned to the east, focusing on Babylonia. The people in the capital city of Babylon were unhappy at this time because their king, Nabonidus, had not been honoring their chief god, Marduk, in the annual New Year's festival. Nabonidus had left Babylon in 530 B.C. and had not returned for almost 10 years. When he did, he brought into Babylon all the statues of the gods from neighboring cities. This only further hardened the feelings of the Babylonians against their king.

Welcomed by the Babylonians

Cyrus quickly seized control of the provinces of Babylonia. His general, Gobryas, then entered Babylon in 539 B.C.

and the city surrendered without a fight. When Cyrus arrived, the Babylonians greeted him not as a conqueror but as a liberator, spreading green branches on the ground before him.

In 586 B.C. the Babylonian king Nebuchadnezzar had destroyed Jerusalem and had taken many of its Jewish inhabitants prisoners. Cyrus's first act was to free these Jews who had been long held captive in Babylon. He not only allowed them to return safely to Palestine (present-day Israel), but he helped rebuild the temple in Jerusalem ruined by Nebuchadnezzar. Cyrus was equally generous to the Babylonians. He returned the statues of the gods Nabonidus had taken and restored many temples in Babylon. He even had his own son, Cambyses II, lead the New Year's festival in 538 B.C.

Cyrus allowed the people in all areas governed by the Persian Empire to worship their own gods and to follow their own customs. They were also allowed to control part of their local governments as long as they paid tributes (taxes) to the empire. With these riches, Cyrus built magnificent buildings in Pasargadae, including a tower-like temple. In 529 B.C., while campaigning in the distant northeastern part of his realm, Cyrus was killed in battle. His body was carried a thousand miles back to Pasargadae and placed in a tomb in his palace.

King David

Israelite king
Ruled 1010-970 B.C.

D avid is described as one of the greatest Israelite kings in the Old Testament of the Bible. He was a warrior, a lawgiver, a musician, and a poet. There are many stories that show he was both a skillful fighter and a tender judge. Although he is depicted as a great king in the Bible, David was not without fault. Many times he lied to or deceived people to get what he wanted. Because he was favored by Yahweh, the Hebrew God, he was not punished directly for his mistakes. Instead, suffering was placed on his children, which in many ways hurt David more. But he was not discouraged from helping his people. With his skill and with Yahweh's aid, David was able to unite the warring tribes of Israel.

Long before David lived, when the Israelites first went to the Promised Land from Egypt, (**see Moses**) Israel was governed by judges. One of the most famous of these was Samuel. When Samuel grew old, his sons took over the position of judge. Since they were untrustworthy, the Israelites asked Samuel to select a king. He did not think he should, since Yah-

"With his skill and with Yahweh's aid, David was able to unite the warring tribes of Israel."

weh was considered the Israelites' true king. The people, however, did not agree. So Samuel anointed, or chose with Yahweh's approval, Saul, who became the first Israelite king.

At first, Saul was successful as king. His army defeated both the Ammonites and the Philistines, enemies of the Israelites. Saul angered Yahweh and Samuel, though. He did not kill his son, Jonathan, who unknowingly disobeyed his order that no troops were to eat before battle. Sparing his son meant breaking an oath made before Yahweh. Saul also did not kill Agag, the captured king of another enemy, the Amalekites, as Samuel (Yahweh's spokesperson) had instructed him to do. So Yahweh directed Samuel to find another king: David.

Samuel Anoints David King

David, the son of Jesse, was a shepherd boy who lived in Bethlehem. After Samuel secretly anointed him, David went to Saul to act as his harp player. He then offered to fight Goliath, the Philistine giant no one would battle. Armed with only a slingshot and a single stone, David killed the giant. The Israelites honored David, which made Saul jealous. This jealously lasted for the rest of Saul's life.

David became commander of the Israelite army, and under him Israel won battle after battle. When Saul's daughter, Michal, fell in love with David, Saul agreed to their marriage only if David accomplished certain tasks against their enemy, the Philistines. He thought David would certainly be killed. When David returned after successfully completing his tasks, Saul became even angrier. He then decided to murder David. But Saul's son Jonathan (who was David's friend) and Michal helped David escape from the city.

Saul tried to hunt down David, but he failed. Many times David could have killed Saul, but he chose not to. For example, there is a story where Saul was chasing David through the wilderness. When Saul stopped in a cave to rest, David, who had been hiding in the cave, crept up on Saul and cut off the corner of his robe. Saul did not notice. As he began to leave the cave, David jumped from the shadows and shouted to the king that he could have killed him. David said he did not do so because he held no grudge against him.

Although Saul still chased David, he soon had to stop in order to prepare to fight the Philistines, who were planning to attack. It was Saul's last battle. His army was defeated, and Jonathan was killed. Saul, who was badly wounded, fell on his sword so he would not be captured. After David mourned Saul's and Jonathan's deaths, he took his newly formed army and accepted kingship over Judah, in the southern part of Palestine. Saul's other sons controlled Israel, just to the north. The two groups soon fought a civil war. With his military skill and Yahweh's support, David was victorious. He brought the two warring kingdoms together and became ruler over both.

Jerusalem Becomes the City of David

It was important, then, for David to make the city of Jerusalem the capital of Israel, since it would link the two former kingdoms together. First he had to defeat the Jebusites, a tribe that lived in the city. Using his personal army, David attacked Jerusalem and captured it. From that time on Jerusalem became known as the City of David.

Into the city David brought the Ark of the Covenant (a wooden box containing Yahweh's commands), which was the Israelites' main icon (religious object). As the Ark was paraded through the city, David danced wildly before it, praising Yahweh. Michal scolded David for what she thought was foolish behavior. As a punishment for criticizing David and not praising Yahweh herself, Michal was not able to bear children the rest of her life.

Although David had many other wives and many children, he desired Bathsheba—a woman who was also married. David, therefore, sent her husband, Uriah, into battle, and Uriah was killed. For his wrongdoing, David was criticized sharply by the prophet Nathan. Once again, since Yahweh favored him, David did not suffer. The son Bathsheba gave birth to, however, died.

David's other children also suffered as a result of his selfishness. David's eldest son, Amnon, raped his half-sister Tamar. Then Tamar's brother Absalom murdered Amnon and left the city. David forgave him, but Absalom rebelled against his father, starting his own army to defeat David and take over Jerusalem. David did not want Absalom harmed, but when the two armies met, Absalom was killed by David's general, Joab.

As he grew older, David grew more gentle and humble. He faced many more wars with the Philistines, but was never defeated in battle. He made the borders of Israel safe for his people. Because Yahweh took pleasure in David, Bathsheba bore him another son, Solomon. It was to Solomon that David passed his strong, united Israelite kingdom.

Fujiwara Michinaga

*Leading member of the
Fujiwara family of Japan*

Born 966

Died 1028

The Heian period in Japanese history, from 794-1185, was a glorious era. Japanese society had grown in the years before this period, but mostly because of the influence of China. The culture of China was much more advanced at this time and Japanese ambassadors, after studying in China, returned to introduce it to their fellow countrymen. With the beginning of the Heian period, however, a distinctive Japanese culture evolved. A written language was developed and unique forms of Japanese art and architecture came into existence. A particular system also formed in Japanese politics. The Fujiwara family, an important aristocratic family, rose to dominate the Japanese government for almost three centuries. The Fujiwaras reached the height of their power during the career of Fujiwara Michinaga.

The original name of the Fujiwara family was Nakatomi. In 645 Nakatomi Kamatari took part in overthrowing the ruling Soga clan and replacing it with a government based on Chinese ideas. The new emperor, grateful for Kamatari's help,

*"The Fujiwara family,
an important
aristocratic family, rose
to dominate the
Japanese government
for almost three
centuries."*

bestowed on him a new family name: Fujiwara. This name may be translated as "wisteria plain," a reference to the spot where the attack on the Soga clan was planned.

Fujiwaras Gain Control Through "Marriage Politics"

After that time, the Fujiwara family wielded considerable influence in the Japanese government. They grew even more powerful over the years as emperors granted them tax-free lands in exchange for their support. By the mid-800s, they were the most powerful family in the imperial court. The Fujiwaras then established almost absolute control in the government through a system referred to as "marriage politics." Under this system, a daughter of the Fujiwara family was married to an emperor. When a child was born to this couple, the emperor was forced to resign and the child was placed on the throne. The head of the Fujiwara family (usually the grandfather) then assumed the role of *sessho* or regent (the person who ruled until the child came of proper age).

The first Fujiwara to become a *sessho* was Fujiwara Yoshifusa in 858. The next leader of the family, Fujiwara Motosune, gained even further control by becoming a *kampaku* or head minister to an adult emperor in 880. Emperors were mostly concerned with court functions and rituals (a practice that continues to the present day). The actual running of the government was done by the emporers' ministers, and the leading ministers for centuries were Fujiwaras. Because of this, the latter part of the Heian period is also referred to as the Fujiwara period.

Fujiwara Michinaga was born in 966, the fourth son of Fujiwara Kaneie and his wife, Tokihime. Initially, Michinaga's chances for attaining a high government position were not good. His father was several places down in the line of succession to power. However, Kaneie proved to be politically skillful. He cleverly arranged for one of his daughters to marry an emperor. When she bore a male heir, the ruling emperor was removed and the child was placed on the throne. Since he was the grandfather, Kaneie became *sessho* in 986.

Politics and Fate Bring Michinaga to Power

As the youngest son, Michinaga still did not have a direct line to power. In 987 he married Rinshi, the daughter of a high-ranking court official. He increased his standing in the government through this marriage and by having his daughters marry other court officials. Kaneie died in 990 and his eldest son assumed the role of *kampaku*. Within five years, however, this son and Michinaga's other brothers all died. A power struggle followed between Michinaga and his cousin (the eldest son of his eldest brother). In 996 this cousin was banished from the government for having committed a minor crime. The emperor at this time decided not to fill the office of *kampaku* and Michinaga was left to continue working behind the scenes.

Even though he did not have an official government title, Michinaga's influence in the affairs of the government was greater then any previous member of his family. He was also an important sponsor of art and culture, and some of the greatest artistic works of the Heian period were produced during this time. Murasaki Shibiku's novel, *Tale of Genji,* written around 1010, is considered one of the world's first and finest novels. Some believe the main character is partly based on Michinaga.

In 1016 the ruling emperor resigned and Michinaga placed his nine-year-old grandson on the throne. He finally had the official title of *sessho.* In order to keep the title in his family, Michinaga turned over the position to his son after only a year. Continuing his power behind the scenes, he worked to maintain his family line to the throne. He was successful. In 1019, with the Fujiwara family's position secure, he joined a Buddhist monastery. He devoted his remaining years to the construction of Hojoji, a great temple and monastery complex in the capital city of Kyoto. Hojoji, one of the finest buildings of the Heian period, was completed in 1022. Six years later, at the age of 62, Michinaga died.

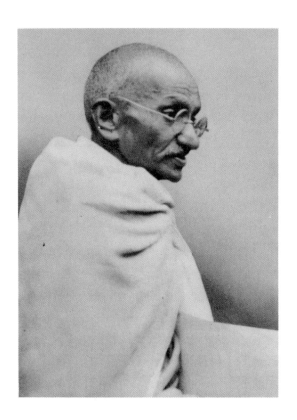

Mohandas Gandhi

Indian political leader

Born October 2, 1869,
Porbandar, Kathiawar, India

Died January 30, 1948,
New Delhi, India

"Gandhi's peaceful approach and ideas helped gain Indian independence and have influenced activists around the world ever since."

England reached the height of its power in the nineteenth century under Queen Victoria (see **Victoria**). Much of its wealth came through the practice of imperialism, the act of taking over another country mostly for economic reasons. England's imperial empire extended over regions from Africa to China, with its largest and most profitable colony the nation of India. Continued English control of this colony, however, was difficult as political movements dedicated to achieving *svaraj* (self-rule) spread through India. Many of these were violent. Mohandas Gandhi worked for Indian independence and unity, but did so through passive (nonviolent) acts of resistance. His peaceful approach and ideas helped gain Indian independence and have influenced activists around the world ever since.

Gandhi's early life gave no clues to his later position as a political leader. He was born in 1869 into a middle-class family in Porbandar, a state in western India. When he was 13, he was married to Kasturbia, with whom he eventually had four sons. In 1887, four years after his marriage, he graduated from high school. Against his wife's and his family's wishes, Gandhi went to London the following year to study law. He returned to India in 1891 to practice law, but was unsuccessful. He left India again after receiving an offer in 1893 to practice in the English-controlled South African province of Natal (in present-day Republic of South Africa). It would be 22 years before he returned.

Experiences Discrimination for the First Time

Gandhi's experience in Natal was a turning point in his life. Over 40,000 Indians resided in Natal, descendants of those brought in by the English to work as laborers. They lived under terrible conditions, and South Africa's English rulers passed racial laws that led to further Indian oppression. Gandhi experienced this prejudice immediately upon his arrival. He was forced out of his first-class train seat after white passengers complained of his presence. This incident shocked Gandhi into action. He began writing pamphlets and journals to bring attention to the discrimination against Indians in South Africa.

At first, Gandhi remained loyal to the English empire, but in 1906 that allegiance turned to anger. The South African government passed an ordinance that year requiring all Indians to register with authorities and to carry that registration at all times. Gandhi reacted by organizing a movement of passive resistance—hunger strikes, mass demonstrations, and marches. This movement, known as *satyagraha* ("holding the truth"), remained the focal point of his activities until his death. Gandhi also rejected western European customs, fully adopting the practices of his native religion of Hinduism. He gave up all his material possessions and dressed in a loincloth and shawl. Because of his protests, Gandhi was arrested and jailed four times.

The South African government finally agreed in 1914 to remove many of the restrictions placed on Indians. The following year Gandhi returned to India to spread his successful message of *satyagraha*. His education and his spiritual conduct appealed to all social classes of Indians. He became known as Mahatma, "great-souled." His appeal was only limited by the many religious differences between Hindus and Muslims that had plagued India for centuries.

During World War I (1914-18), Gandhi supported England in hopes it would grant India freedom after the war. It was not to be. In 1919 England enacted several bills that restricted Indian civil rights. In response, Gandhi called for the first nationwide *satyagraha.* Scattered violence, however, ruined the campaign, and the government quickly struck back. At the city of Amritsar, where an Indian mob had burned banks and railroad stations the day before, government troops machine-gunned a large Indian crowd. In the massacre, 400 Indians were killed and 1,200 were wounded. Horrified by the violence on both sides, Gandhi stopped his campaign for a while, but he never again supported England.

In the early 1920s, Gandhi assumed leadership of a political party, the Indian National Congress. He drafted the party's constitution, which called for Indian independence through peaceful means, and broke all ties the party had with the English. He again declared a *satyagraha,* but it only resulted in mass arrests. Outraged Indians then resorted to violence, burning a police headquarters and killing 21 policemen. After this incident, Gandhi realized his people were not yet ready for passive resistance. He dropped his campaign. Nevertheless, in 1922 he was arrested and jailed for two years.

Leads Salt March to Protest English Authority

In 1928, frustrated by the lack of reforms, Gandhi urged the Indian National Congress to launch another nationwide strike. He hoped it would convince the English to meet Indian demands for independence. It did not. In 1930, to protest the government's heavy tax on salt, Gandhi led a 200-mile march to the Indian Ocean to take salt directly from the sea. This "Salt March" released long-held Indian anger, and a swell of protest and unrest swept across India. Thousands were imprisoned. Gandhi was arrested and jailed.

The 1930s saw little improvement in Indian life. The English government offered various reforms, but never the full freedom that Gandhi demanded. In 1935 the government passed the India Act, allowing Indians to elect representatives to a national legislature. But an English viceroy still led the national government and English governors still managed all the Indian provinces. The Indian National Congress, mostly composed of Hindus, won a majority of the seats in the legislature. This only widened the division between India's Hindus and Muslims, who were represented by the Muslim League. Fearing the Hindus would take control if India gained independence, the Muslim League called for the creation of the separate Muslim state of Pakistan.

Believing India could become free only if it were united, Gandhi worked to bring the two parties together. However, World War II (1939-45) destroyed his efforts. The Muslim League supported England's war effort, but the Indian National

Mohandas Gandhi, at age 78, fasting for peace in January 1948.

Congress refused to do so until independence was granted. Siding with the Congress, Gandhi called for a renewed *satyagraha* in October of 1940. He was arrested and jailed. In 1942 England promised to grant India independence as soon as the war ended if all Indians supported the war effort. Gandhi found this offer worthless and organized his last *satyagraha,* the "Quit India" campaign. He was arrested and jailed until 1944.

Although Gandhi remained a spiritual leader among the Indians, his political influence decreased. Hindus and Muslims grew further apart and neither group listened to Gandhi's pleas to remain united. In 1947, after England finally granted independence, the country was divided into two separate nations—India for the Hindus and Pakistan for the Muslims. Riots immediately broke out between the two religious groups, leaving over one million people dead. Gandhi toured troubled areas and promised to fast until Hindus and Muslims reached peace. On January 30, 1948, while walking to a prayer meeting, Gandhi was shot and killed by a Hindu fanatic.

Genghis Khan

Mongolian chieftain
Born c. 1162
Died 1227

Before the thirteenth century, Mongols were nomadic (wandering) people who lived in present-day northern China, Mongolia, and southern Russia. The Mongols were skilled horsemen and fierce fighters who raided farmlands and villages, usually destroying everything they did not take. Gathered into numerous tribes, they more often fought among themselves. A leader finally arose to bring these scattered, warring tribes together to form a nation. His name was Genghis Khan. Under his command, the Mongols turned their unforgiving arms against the rest of Asia. In less than 20 years, he controlled an immense empire stretching across the middle of Asia from the Sea of Japan west to the Black Sea. No single man in history conquered as much of the world as Khan, and no man's name was feared as much.

Legend states that when Genghis Khan was born around 1162, he came into the world holding a lump of clotted blood. Among the Mongols, this was viewed as a sign of a future warrior. He was named Temujin by his father, Yesugei, a

"No single man in history conquered as much of the world as Khan, and no man's name was feared as much."

chieftain over various Mongol tribes. When Temujin was nine years old, he was promised in marriage to Borte, the daughter of a nearby chieftain. When Yesugei was returning from the feast celebrating this future marriage, he was poisoned by a band of Tartars (Tatars). The Tartars, a nomadic tribe who probably originated in central Siberia, had long been sworn enemies of the Mongols.

With Yesugei's death, Temujin was in control. The opposing tribes in his camp did not want to be led by a young boy, but killing him would have started a feud with his relatives. Instead, the other leaders abandoned Temujin and his family on the desolate plains outside the camp. For five years the family was forced to live on wild plants, birds, fish, mice, and any other small animals they could kill. Despite these harsh conditions, Temujin survived and grew strong. When he was about 14, one Mongol tribe learned of his existence and captured him. He quickly escaped.

Gains Allies Through Personality and Diplomacy

Temujin soon showed the traits that would benefit him throughout his life: charisma and shrewdness. Wherever he went, Temujin attracted warriors who gave up everything to follow him and who remained loyal to him even after defeat in battle. He gained the allegiance of others through his diplomatic skills. When he was 15, he claimed his bride, Borte, and received a splendid fur cloak from her father. Recognizing the value of the cloak, Temujin presented it to Toghrul, chieftain of the Karait tribe and a former ally of Yesugei. Pleased with the gift, Toghrul pledged his loyalty to Temujin.

Around 1184 Borte was stolen by warriors from the Merkit tribe. Toghrul agreed to help Temujin retrieve her and also called in Jamukha, chief of the Jairat tribe. Temujin only had a few warriors in his camp, but quickly rounded up more. The Merkit were routed in the ensuing battle and Borte was rescued. Those Merkit who chose to follow Temujin were spared and given a place in his camp. Following the battle, Temujin and Jamukha exchanged the oath of *anda,* becoming

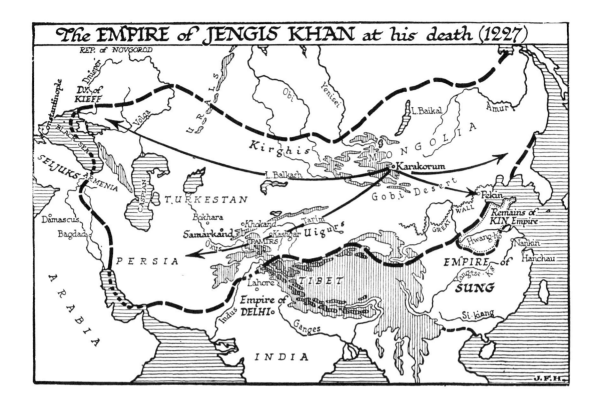

The EMPIRE of JENGIS KHAN at his death (1227)

blood brothers. For a year, they housed their two armies in the same camp. Temujin's growing control over the camp, however, upset Jamukha and he broke away. Shortly afterward, several major tribes in Jamukha's group defected to Temujin. The two blood brothers soon became hated enemies.

Temujin's reputation and strength increased as he conquered fellow Mongol tribesmen. Fearing Temujin's power, Jamukha persuaded Toghrul to join him and others against Temujin. It proved to be a fatal decision. In 1203 Toghrul's forces attacked and nearly wiped out Temujin's army. A few months later, Temujin took his revenge. After assembling almost 6,000 warriors, Temujin ambushed the camp of the elderly chieftain in the dead of night. After three days of fighting, the Keraits were destroyed. In the spring of the following year, Temujin and his army battled the Naiman tribe near the Kerulan River in present-day northeast Mongolia. Jamukha's personal forces were allied with the Naiman, and Temujin was badly outnumbered. But his troops fought fiercely and mercilessly, and the Naiman and Jamukha's men were slaughtered. Jamukha escaped, only to be captured and killed several months later.

Becomes "Genghis Khan"

In 1206 Temujin was proclaimed ruler of all the Mongol tribes and given the title Genghis Khan ("encompassing ruler"). The Mongols were united for the first time in their history. Khan then set about building his empire. His battle tactics were simple: the Mongols wore down their enemies by sending wave after wave of attackers. If enemies surrendered, their lives and property were spared, but if they did not, the Mongols destroyed everything in sight.

In 1213 the Mongols climbed over the Great Wall of China and attacked the army of the Chin empire of northern China. Within two years Khan controlled most of its territory and its capital, Yenching (present-day Beijing). He then turned his forces westward, conquering the present-day regions of Turkistan and Transoxiana in 1218. Over the next seven years, the Mongols swept through the present-day countries of Afghanistan, Iran, and Azerbaijan. They climbed over the Caucasus Mountains along the southern border of present-day Russia and stood on the eastern shores of the Black Sea.

In 1225 Khan returned to present-day Mongolia to conquer the remaining territories in northern China. While fighting this campaign, he fell from his horse, fatally injuring himself. He died in 1227. Legend states that when Khan was buried, 40 beautiful maidens and 40 horses were slaughtered at his grave. Under his son, Ogodei, the Mongols continued expanding their empire.

Haile Selassie I

Ethiopian emperor
Born July 23, 1892,
Harar, Ethiopia
Died August 27, 1975,
Addis Ababa, Ethiopia

Haile Selassie I led Ethiopia for nearly 60 years. Before World War II (1939-45), he helped modernize the country. He established schools and hospitals, improved transportation and communication, and strengthened the central government. When Italy, led by the dictator Benito Mussolini, invaded Ethiopia in 1935, Haile Selassie personally led the Ethiopian army in battle. After World War II, he became a leading voice in African affairs, making Ethiopia a center for the Organization of African Unity. The great improvements that marked his early reign, however, were not matched in his later period. Hungry for quicker reforms, Ethiopians stripped him of his powers and forced him from the throne.

Haile Selassie was born Tafari Makonnen in 1892 in Harar, the capital of the Ethiopian province of Harar. He was the son of Ras Makonnen and Yeshi-immabet Ali. Besides being governor of the province, Ras Makonnen was a first cousin and a close advisor to Menelik II, the emperor of

"After World War II, Haile Selassie became a leading voice in African affairs, making Ethiopia a center for the Organization of African Unity."

Ethiopia. Because he was a brilliant student, quickly becoming fluent in several languages, the young Tafari was soon granted many ruling positions by Menelik II. In 1907 he became a *dejazmach* or earl. A year later he was appointed governor of the large southern province of Sidamo. When his father died in 1910, Tafari became governor of his home province of Harar. The following year, he married Menen Asfaw, the niece of Lij Yasu, who was the heir to the throne.

Lij Yasu became emperor in 1913, but most Ethiopians opposed him. While the majority of people in the country were Christians, he was a Muslim. Leading the forces against Lij Yasu, Tafari organized a plot that overthrew the young emperor in 1916. Lij Yasu's young daughter, Zauditu, became the new empress with Tafari serving as her regent (the person who would rule in her place until she came of age).

Once in power, Tafari enacted a host of domestic reforms. He increased educational opportunities by founding schools throughout Ethiopia and by allowing Ethiopians to travel to other countries to study. To establish a stable source of income for Ethiopia, he placed taxes on foreign goods coming into the country. He had new hospitals built and founded a newspaper, which helped Ethiopian farmers by discussing modern agricultural techniques.

Brings Ethiopia to the World Stage

Tafari's greatest work during this time came in foreign affairs. Through his lobbying, Ethiopia was unanimously elected in 1923 to the League of Nations, an international organization formed in 1919 to promote peace and cooperation between countries. In 1924 Tafari further enhanced Ethiopia's worldwide standing by visiting Egypt and several countries in Europe. This marked the first time an Ethiopian leader had ever traveled abroad.

In 1928 Tafari convinced Empress Zauditu to grant him the title of *negus* or king. When Zauditu died two years later, Tafari was crowned the new emperor. He took the name Haile Selassie, which in the Ethiopian language of Amharic means "power of the Trinity." He quickly moved to create a more centralized government system in Ethiopia. He divided his kingdom into 12 provinces and 75 sub-provinces, appointing trusted friends as governors of these areas. To strengthen the army, he founded a military academy and brought in foreign advisors to train his new officers. In 1931 he offered Ethiopia its first constitution. Although this constitution called for the formation of a parliament (a legislative body), it allowed Haile Selassie to retain almost absolute authority in the government.

Haile Selassie's reforms were disrupted by an Italian invasion in 1935. Wanting to control the entire area around the Red Sea, Benito Mussolini launched a full-scale war, including poison gas raids, against the weaker Ethiopians. Haile Selassie personally led his army into battle, but it was defeated and he had to flee to Europe in 1936. He then went before the League of Nations. In an eloquent and emotional speech, Haile Selassie pleaded with member nations to come to Ethiopia's aid. They responded with weak economic sanctions against Italy that did nothing to help Ethiopia. By the end of 1937 Mussolini had conquered the Ethiopians.

With English military aid, Haile Selassie was finally able to regain his throne in 1941. In the nearly ruined Ethiopia, he tried to reestablish his reforms over the next twenty years, but was not quite successful. In 1955 he introduced a revised constitution that permitted popular election of members to a national assembly. However, he resisted attempts to create a truly democratic government, retaining the power to appoint almost all major officials.

Works for African Unity

In the 1960s and 1970s, Haile Selassie focused his attention on African concerns. Along with other African leaders, he established the Organization of African Unity in 1963 in the Ethiopian capital of Addis Ababa. Composed of 32 independent African nations, this organization promoted educational, scientific, and political cooperation among its members. As a peacemaker, Haile Selassie helped end civil wars in Nigeria (1970) and in Sudan (1972).

While he worked for change in the rest of Africa at this time, Haile Selassie moved slowly in his own country. He could not ease the continued tensions between Christians and Muslims in Ethiopia. Neither could he solve the problem of poverty that continually affected the rural areas of his country. Haile Selassie's failure to react to a devastating famine in northern Ethiopia in 1973 finally resulted in his downfall. Ethiopians responded with strikes and demonstrations, and junior officers in the government quickly seized power. Haile Selassie was forced from the throne in September 1974, spending the remaining year of his life under house arrest. He died alone on August 27, 1975.

Hammurabi

King of Babylon in ancient Mesopotamia
Ruled c. 1792-1759 B.C.

Mesopotamia was an ancient region in southwest Asia that occupied the area between the Tigris and Euphrates rivers. It extended north from the head of the present-day Persian Gulf to the mountains in present-day Armenia. In Greek, Mesopotamia literally means "between the rivers." Many city-states were included in this region. Among them was Babylon, located about 50 miles south of present-day Baghdad, Iraq, on the Euphrates river. Under the reign of Hammurabi, who came to power almost 3,800 years ago, Babylon rose to prominence. It became the capital of his empire of Babylonia, which spread over much of Mesopotamia. A just king, Hammurabi is best remembered for developing the Code of Hammurabi, a set of 282 laws controlling almost all aspects of Babylonian society.

When Hammurabi succeeded his father, Sin-muballit, to the throne of Babylon around 1792 B.C., the kingdom was small—only 80 miles long and 20 miles wide. Larger states with more powerful kings surrounded Babylon. Seven years

Hammurabi's "greatest achievement was the establishment of law and order in Babylonia."

into his rule, Hammurabi started to expand his kingdom. He conquered the neighboring cities of Uruk and Isin, and then, two years later, the small country of Emutbal. For an 18-year period after this, Hammurabi ruled in relative peace. He improved the cities of his kingdom and built and restored many temples.

Beginning around 1764 B.C., a number of neighboring cites from the northeast banded together to attack Hammurabi. He defeated them handily. With his empire strengthened by these victories, he moved against his old enemy to the south, the powerful Rim-Sin of Larsa. This time Hammurabi emerged triumphant. By 1762 B.C., his empire of Babylonia was supreme in all of southern and central Mesopotamia.

Creates Code to Help Poor and Oppressed

Hammurabi was more than a military king bent on conquest. He personally supervised almost all aspects of his kingdom: the digging of canals, the building of religious temples, even the revising of the calendar. His greatest achievement was the establishment of law and order in Babylonia. He was greatly concerned with helping the poor and oppressed in his kingdom, and issued many laws and regulations protecting them. Near the end of his reign, Hammurabi had these laws carved into a stone column for all his subjects to read.

The Code of Hammurabi is the longest-surviving text from this period of history in Mesopotamia. The column was discovered almost completely intact in southwestern Iran by French archaeologists in 1901. It is now preserved in the Louvre Museum in Paris, France. At the top of this seven-foot column is a scene of Hammurabi praying before Shamash, the Babylonian god of the sun and of justice. Under this scene is a Prologue written by Hammurabi giving his reasons for developing the Code, including "to cause justice to prevail in the land." The laws are carved under the Prologue, both on the front and the back of the column. Everything is written in cuneiform, wedge-shaped characters used to represent words or ideas.

The 282 laws deal with a wide range of social matters: marriage, divorce, private property, wages, trade, theft, assault, slavery, and many others. Hammurabi's laws were not the first such "code" created in the ancient world. Their emphasis on justice, however, was an advance over previous rules.

Code Sets Down Harsh Justice

Two characteristics marked the Code of Hammurabi. The first was the *lex talionis,* or the practice of giving a punishment equal to the crime committed. For example, law number 196 stated that "If a man has put out the eye of another man, they shall put out his eye." The second characteristic was the extreme harshness of the penalties, which included drowning, burning, and other mutilations.

Three basic social classes existed in Babylonia under Hammurabi, and the Code reflected this. *Awilum* were free men (the highest class), *mushkenum* were citizens responsible to the government, and *wardum* were slaves. Punishments were given out according to one's social rank. If an *awilum* lost an eye, then the aggressor also lost an eye. If the victim were a *mushkenum,* however, the aggressor only had to pay the victim a fee. The aggressor paid even less if the victim were a *wardum.*

Justice, however, was the main concern of the Code. The very first law stated that "If a man accuses another man of murder and it proves to be false, the accuser shall be put to death." Other laws dealing with family and property protected women and children from poverty and neglect. A man was allowed to divorce his wife, but if he had children, he had to continue to support both his wife and his children.

The empire of Babylonia did not last long after Hammurabi's death. Kassites, tribesmen from the Zagros Mountains to the east, attacked and defeated his son, Samsuiluna. The capital city of Babylon was eventually burned to the ground. Although Hammurabi had instructed future kings to pay attention to his great Code, its influence can never be truly measured. There are no historical references to its continued use.

Hannibal

Carthaginian general

Born 247 B.C.,
Carthage

Died 183 B.C.,
Bithynia, present-day Turkey

"Hannibal was a brilliant and courageous general who lived for one purpose: to eliminate the power of Rome."

Rome had conquered all of Italy by the first half of the third century B.C. It then began its quest for power in the regions around the Mediterranean Sea. The city-state of Carthage on the northeast coast of present-day Tunisia controlled almost all of the western Mediterranean, making it Rome's chief opponent. Over the next century, Rome and Carthage struggled in battles that came to be known as the Punic Wars. With its generals, its great military, and its economic resources, Rome was clearly favored in the struggle. But Carthage had a military commander who, to this day, has had few equals. Hannibal was a brilliant and courageous general who lived for one purpose: to eliminate the power of Rome. He almost succeeded.

Hannibal was the son of Hamilcar Barca, a Carthaginian commander who had fought in the First Punic War (264-241 B.C.). Hamilcar had defended parts of Sicily, an island off the southern coast of Italy, against Roman conquest. Hamilcar made his son swear from an early age to hate Rome forever.

Hannibal never broke that promise. Hamilcar was assassinated in 228 B.C. while trying to hold on to Carthaginian power in Spain. Hannibal's brother-in-law, Hasdrubal the Splendid, then assumed command. Upon his assassination seven years later, the Carthaginian army chose Hannibal to lead it.

Before his death, Hasdrubal the Splendid had negotiated a treaty with Rome that established a border between Roman and Carthaginian regions. The city of Saguntum, on the eastern coast of Spain, fell within Carthaginian control, but allied itself with the Romans. In 219 B.C. Hannibal and his army attacked Saguntum. The siege lasted eight months before the city surrendered. When Hannibal refused to release the city, Rome declared the beginning of the Second Punic War, sometimes called the Hannibalic War.

Incredible Climb Through the Alps

Hannibal did not wait for the Romans to attack. He set out to invade Rome. In the spring of 218 B.C., he led his small army, along with 40 elephants, across the Pyrenees (mountain range on the French-Spanish border) and into the valley of the Rhone River in eastern France. There Roman scouts learned of Hannibal's movements. Not yet wanting to battle the Romans, Hannibal and his men pushed into the Alps. It was early autumn and the steep, narrow trails through the mountains were already covered with snow and ice. Some of the Carthaginians and most of the elephants did not survive. Yet, in the span of only two weeks, Hannibal and the majority of his men emerged from the Alps.

In the valley of the Ticino River in present-day southern Switzerland, Hannibal met a Roman army under the command of Publius Cornelius Scipio. This first battle in the Second Punic War ended in a Carthaginian victory. The Romans quickly retreated and Hannibal and his men took up defensive positions along the Trebbia River in northwest Italy. Scipio and his forces attacked again. This time, they were nearly wiped out by Hannibal's army. While Scipio and the remaining Romans headed south, the Carthaginians spent the winter near the river.

In the spring of 217 B.C., Hannibal led his troops across the Apennines (a mountain range in central Italy) and toward Rome. Avoiding contact with the main Roman army, Hannibal marched through the defenseless countryside. He destroyed cities, gathering food and supplies as he went. Finally, at Lake Trasimene, Hannibal encountered the Romans under Caius Flaminius. The Carthaginian army, perched on higher ground, swept down and surrounded the Romans, killing thousands.

Crushes Romans at Cannae

After this defeat, the Romans held off attacking Hannibal, thinking his supplies would soon run out. But in 216 B.C., under new leadership, the Roman army pursued Hannibal and his men to the village of Cannae in southeast Italy. It was a mistake. Hannibal had positioned his men in an arc with the sun and wind at their backs. Blinded, the Romans walked into the center of Hannibal's army and his two outer flanks closed around them. Tens of thousands of Romans were slaughtered. Cannae was the worst defeat ever for Rome.

Despite this crushing victory, Hannibal could not advance on Rome. Because Carthage did not send needed supplies, his army had to attack and raid smaller cities. For the next few years, the Romans and the Carthaginians traded victories in battle. Soon the Romans gained the upper hand. The son of Publius Cornelius Scipio, who came to be known as Scipio Africanus Major, led a Roman army to the Metaurus River in central Italy in 207 B.C. There he met an army led by Hannibal's brother Hasdrubal. After routing the Carthaginians, Scipio Africanus beheaded Hasdrubal. He then had the severed head rushed south and tossed into Hannibal's camp. Without Hasdrubal's aid, Hannibal was forced to retreat into the granite mountains of Bruttium in southern Italy.

Hannibal had to travel back to Carthage in 203 B.C. to stop the advance of Scipio Africanus. The following year the two met at the battle of Zama, southwest of Carthage, where the Roman forces soundly defeated the Carthaginians. A treaty was signed in 201 B.C., ending the Second Punic War. Hannibal returned to Carthage, but the Romans continued to harass him.

Over the next twenty years, he sought protection in country after country. In 183 B.C. the Romans cornered him in Bithynia (an ancient country in present-day northwest Turkey). Instead of surrendering to the Romans and spending the rest of his life in jail, Hannibal drank poison.

Hatshepsut

Egyptian queen who ruled as a pharaoh

Born c. 1520 B.C.,
Egypt

Died c. 1468 B.C.,
Egypt

> *"Hatshepsut's reign was distinguished not by battles and conquest but by peace and artistry."*

Ancient Egypt reached the height of its civilization during the Eighteenth Dynasty, which ran from about 1570 B.C. to 1340 B.C. This period also marks the beginning of what is termed the New Empire or New Kingdom in the history of Egypt. The pharaohs (rulers) of the Eighteenth Dynasty conquered territory in Asia as far east as the Euphrates River in present-day Syria. They also erected great buildings and temples around the capital city of Thebes. Hatshepsut was the sole female ruler during this period. Her reign was distinguished not by battles and conquest but by peace and artistry. Although later male kings tried to erase her memory, she is recognized today as one of the greatest female leaders of the ancient world.

Hatshepsut was the oldest of two daughters born to Pharaoh Thutmose I and Queen Ahmose. Since she was female, Hatshepsut could not legally claim her father's throne. Therefore, at an early age, she was forced to marry her half-brother Thutmose II in order to strengthen his claim to the throne. The two began ruling Egypt around 1495 B.C., but Thutmose II died unexpectedly after only a few years. Since he and Hatshepsut had no sons of their own, his son by a woman in his harem assumed the throne. Thutmose III, however, was only ten years old at the time, and Hatshepsut had to rule Egypt as his regent (the person who ruled in his place until he came of age).

A year after becoming regent, Hatshepsut sent a large expedition south of Thebes to the stone quarries of Syene (present-day Aswan). She instructed her subjects to return with two red granite obelisks (four-sided pillars that taper off at the top into a pyramid). To bring back these huge 185-foot obelisks, a 300-foot barge had to be built. Twenty-seven other ships, containing 864 oarsmen, then pulled this barge up the Nile River to Thebes. Once there, the obelisks were covered with gold and set up in nearby Karnak in the Temple of Amon-Ra (the supreme god of ancient Egypt), which still stands today.

Crowns Herself King

Hatshepsut proclaimed herself "king" of Egypt shortly after this. She gave herself all the powers and all the titles that went with the throne. She was portrayed on public monuments throughout the empire in the full outfit of a male pharaoh: royal skirt, ceremonial beard, and a crown. Beyond this, however, she was clearly shown to be female.

Around 1480 B.C., Hatshepsut sent a peaceful trading expedition to the country of Punt, which was probably located along the northern coast of present-day Somalia. In ancient times, Punt was famous for its incense and other exotic goods. In exchange for jewelry and weapons, the Puntites gave the Egyptians aromatic herbs, leopard skins, live animals, gold, ebony, and myrrh trees. After this visit, Egypt and Punt enjoyed a trading relationship for many years.

Builds Temple at Deir el–Bahri

At this same time, Hatshepsut began work on the most important of her monuments—her famous mortuary (funeral) temple at Deir el-Bahri in western Thebes. The terraced temple, which still exists, is set into the rocks of the surrounding cliffs and built almost entirely of limestone. Although never completed, the temple contains many painted reliefs on its walls. These depict Hatshepsut's supposed divine birth, the transport of the first set of obelisks from Syene to Thebes, and the successful trading expedition to Punt.

Hatshepsut sent a second expedition to cut another pair of obelisks at the quarries of Syene around 1475 B.C. Unlike the first pair, only the upper portions of these were covered in gold. One of this second pair of obelisks still stands in the Temple of Amon-Ra: it is 97 feet tall and weighs 320 tons. During these later years of her reign, Hatshepsut revived the turquoise mines the Egyptians had built in the Sinai Peninsula. This semi-precious stone was used for jewelry and for decorating the temples.

Hatshepsut suddenly disappears from Egyptian records around 1468 B.C. What became of her remains a mystery. She ruled for almost 20 years and may have simply died a natural death. After her death or disappeance, however, her statues were destroyed, her temples were walled up, and her name was removed from buildings throughout Egypt. Later male kings tried to ignore her very existence, but her name and her accomplishments have endured through the centuries.

Ho Chi Minh

President of North Vietnam

*Born May 19, 1890,
Kim Lien, Vietnam*

*Died September 3, 1969,
Hanoi, North Vietnam*

Imperialism, the act of one country taking over another mostly for economic reasons, reached its height during the late nineteenth century. It was spurred on by the Industrial Revolution, the rapid development of machinery and industries in Europe in the late eighteenth and early nineteenth centuries. European countries soon raced to find greater markets for their goods and more materials to fuel their industries. In its grab for land and resources, France took control of areas in southeast Asia, which it called Indochina (present-day Cambodia, Laos, and Vietnam). From an early age, Ho Chi Minh was among those in Vietnam who rebelled against the French rule. He was the founder of the Vietnamese Communist Party and was its leader for almost 40 years. Ho secured Vietnam's independence from France and later led the fight to unify the country under Communism.

Ho was born Nguyen That Thanh in 1890 in the village of Kim Lien in central Vietnam. His father, Nguyen Sinh Sac, was a local government official and educator who protested

"Ho secured Vietnam's independence from France and later led the fight to unify the country under Communism."

against French domination in Vietnam. In 1908 Ho attended the National Academy in the nearby city of Hué, but was expelled because he took part in anti-French protests. After working as a schoolteacher in a small southern village, he left Vietnam in 1911 as a cook aboard a French steamship. At sea for two years, Ho visited ports in Africa, Europe, and the United States, and learned to speak Chinese, French, Russian, English, and Thai.

Influenced by Ideas of Lenin

During World War I (1914-18), Ho worked as a cook in London, England, and as a photo retoucher in Paris, France. While in France, he learned of the social ideas of the Russian Communist leader Vladimir Lenin (see **Vladimir Lenin**). Impressed, Ho helped found the French Communist party in 1920. A few years later he traveled to Moscow to study Communist philosophy at the University of Oriental Workers. He was then sent in 1925 to Canton, China, to organize a Communist movement.

In 1930, at a meeting in Hong Kong, Ho founded the Indochinese Communist Party (ICP), made up of revolutionaries from Indochina. Because of his political activities, he was arrested by English authorities in Hong Kong and jailed for two years. After he was released in 1933, Ho traveled back to Moscow where he remained for several years, reportedly recovering from tuberculosis.

At the outbreak of World War II (1939-45), Japan invaded and occupied Vietnam. Under the name Ho Chi Minh ("He Who Shines"), Ho returned to Vietnam in 1941 to organize resistance to the Japanese and French. Along with leaders of the ICP, he formed the Viet Minh, an organization to work for Vietnamese independence. From 1941 to 1945, Ho built up the Viet Minh's guerrilla army for an uprising at the end of the war. When the war in the Pacific ended in August 1945, Viet Minh forces launched an attack to seize power in Vietnam. On September 2 Ho proclaimed the creation in the north of the independent Democratic Republic of Vietnam. The city of Hanoi became its capital.

Ends French Rule in Indochina

Trying to regain control of Vietnam, France negotiated with Ho. The talks soon broke down over the issue of who would control the rich southern portion of Vietnam. Warfare began in December 1946 and lasted until 1954, when the French were finally defeated at Dienbienphu in northern Vietnam. This loss marked the end of French rule in Indochina. In July 1954 an agreement was reached calling for the temporary division of Vietnam into a Communist north and a non-Communist south. Ho became the first president of North Vietnam.

The agreement had also called for general elections in 1956. Aimed at reuniting North and South Vietnam, these elections were to be held throughout the country. Fearing that the elections would give control to Ho and the Communists, the government in South Vietnam refused to take part. In 1960 Ho supported the creation in South Vietnam of the National Liberation Front, better known as the Viet Cong. The aim of this resistance movement was to topple the non-Communist government in the south and reunify the country. When clashes erupted between the Viet Cong and the South Vietnamese government, the United States sent military advisors to help South Vietnam. By 1965 the United States was fully committed to the Vietnam War, sending in troops and bombing Communist-controlled areas.

When Ho's health began to decline in the mid-1960s, he reduced his role in the government. He died of an apparent heart attack on September 3, 1969, and was buried in a mausoleum in Hanoi. Less than six years later, the North Vietnamese defeated the American-backed South Vietnamese. Vietnam was formally

The Vietnam War–The U.S. Cost

The United States fought in the Vietnam War from 1961 to 1973. In 1969, at the height of the fighting, more than 500,000 U.S. troops were involved. The length of the war and its casualties—both military and civilian—deeply divided Americans. Those who opposed the war organized huge peace rallies in cities across the country. Some of these rallies turned violent. In 1970, at Kent State University in Ohio, national guardsmen shot and killed four students during an antiwar protest. By the time the United States withdrew from Vietnam in 1973, more than 58,000 U.S. troops had been killed in the war. Hundreds more were listed as missing-in-action. The war cost the United States over $150 billion.

reunited under the Communists in July 1976. To honor Ho, the Communist government renamed Saigon, the former capital of South Vietnam, Ho Chi Minh City.

Irene of Athens

Byzantine empress

Born c. 752,
Athens, Greece

Died 803,
Lesbos

When Irene of Athens was crowned sole ruler of the Byzantine Empire in 797, she became the first woman ever to hold the throne of the old Roman Empire. The Byzantine Empire, also known as the East Roman Empire, was founded by Constantine I (see **Constantine I**) in 330. It was all that remained of the Roman Empire after Rome was sacked in 476. Irene ranks with Egyptian Queen Hatshepsut (see **Hatshepsut**) and Russian Empress Catherine the Great (see **Catherine II, the Great**) as a breaker of male-dominated dynasties. Her illegal claim to the throne allowed the Frank king Charlemagne (see **Charlemagne**) to be crowned Roman emperor in the West. This coronation ended the Byzantine Empire's power in Europe and forever changed European history.

Irene was born around 752 to a noble Greek family of Athens. No information exists about her childhood. It is believed that her beauty alone gained her a marriage in 769 to Leo IV, who became the Byzantine emperor in 775. A year

"Irene ranks with Egyptian Queen Hatshepsut and Russian Empress Catherine the Great as a breaker of male-dominated dynasties."

after they were married, Irene gave birth to a son, Constantine VI. When Leo IV died in 780, Constantine VI became emperor with Irene as his regent (the person who would rule in his place until he came of age).

Controversy Over Icons

Irene came to rule the Byzantine Empire at a time when it was deeply divided over the use of icons (sacred paintings or sculptures) in the church. Constantine I had issued the Edict of Milan in 313 legalizing Christianity in the Roman Empire. Over time, instead of worshiping what the icons represented, more and more people in the Empire began to venerate (regard as holy) the icons themselves. This practice had become so extreme by the eighth century that a movement against icons, called iconoclasm, arose. Supporters of this movement were called iconoclasts. In 730 the Byzantine emperor Leo III destroyed a major icon and issued a decree against the veneration of icons.

Despite this decree, many people continued the practice of venerating icons. Irene was among them. After she became regent, she removed iconoclastic generals and other officials in the Byzantine government. She had Tarasius, one of her supporters, elected head of the Byzantine Church in 784. Together, Irene and Tarasius called together more than 300 bishops to formally reject iconoclasm. At the end of this meeting, known as the Second Council of Nicaea, the bishops declared that icons should be venerated but not worshiped.

When Constantine VI came of age around 790, he was determined to rule for himself. Fearing she would lose power when he came to the throne, Irene demanded that her name be placed above his in all public documents. Constantine VI then planned to remove Irene from the Byzantine capital of Constantinople, but she learned of the plot and had him confined in the palace. Afterward, she ordered the military to swear an oath of allegiance to her as supreme ruler. They rebelled and freed Constantine VI from the palace. Irene and her supporters were arrested and banished from the palace.

Gains Throne By Having Her Son Blinded

In 792, however, Constantine VI pardoned Irene and allowed her to return as empress. Still wanting complete rule, Irene plotted against her son over the next few years. When Constantine VI discovered his mother's treachery, he left Constantinople in 797 to round up loyal troops. He was captured by Irene's forces, however, and brought back to the palace. In the same room where he was born 27 years earlier, Constantine VI was blinded at his mother's orders. He died shortly afterward.

Sitting alone on the Byzantine throne, Irene controlled what was left of the Roman Empire. This, however, presented a problem. Under Roman law, no woman could become commander in chief of the army. Since Roman emperors held this position, no women could legally become emperor. For this reason, Pope Leo III considered the Roman throne to be legally vacant. To fill the seat, he turned to the Frank king Charlemagne, who ruled over most of west and central Europe. In 800 Leo III crowned Charlemagne the Roman emperor in the West, giving him control of the former Roman Empire in Europe. This act officially eliminated the Byzantine Empire from the Roman world.

Irene did not rule effectively. The ministers of her government quarreled among themselves and the military was never fully loyal to her. To gain the favor of her subjects, Irene reduced some taxes and abolished others. This tactic, however, ruined the Byzantine economy. In 802 her high officials plotted against her and placed Nicephorus, the minister of finance, on the throne. Irene was taken to the island of Lesbos in the Aegean Sea off the west coast of Turkey, where she died in 803. Because of her fight for the veneration of icons, the Greek Church today recognizes Irene as a saint.

Jesus of Nazareth

Jewish prophet, teacher, and healer

Born c. 6 B.C.
Bethlehem, Judaea

Died c. A.D. 26
Jerusalem, Judaea

"Wandering throughout Galilee, in the northern part of Palestine, Jesus taught the importance of having faith in God and of having love for mankind."

For 2,000 years Christians have revered Jesus as the Son of God. Even followers of other religions, such as Muslims and Hindus, recognize him as a prophet (one whose words are inspired by God) or as an avatar (a god in human form). But it is almost impossible to separate the historical man from the religious figure in the Bible. Most of the details of his life are not known. What is known about Jesus comes from the first four books of the New Testament, the Gospels according to Matthew, Mark, Luke, and John. These are not, however, historical descriptions of Jesus' life. Written more than 40 years after his death, they are religious accounts of his teachings and the miracles attributed to his life.

To better understand Jesus' life, it is necessary to understand the place and time into which he was born and lived. Palestine was a historic region on the eastern shore of the Mediterranean Sea. It was made up of parts of what are now Israel, Jordan, and Egypt. Around 1200 B.C., Moses (see **Moses**) led the Jewish people out of slavery in Egypt to Palestine. A Jewish kingdom was finally organized there around 1000 B.C. by Saul, which David (see **David**), after him, united. But in 333 B.C., the Macedonian ruler Alexander the Great (see **Alexander the Great**) conquered Palestine. It then came under the rule of the Roman Empire when the Roman general Pompey captured the region in 63 B.C. From that time on, many prophets and healers traveled throughout Palestine. Some urged the Jewish people to protest Roman rule. But others, religious reformers, believed the people were suffering because they had ignored their worship of God.

Into this period of political and religious unrest Jesus was born, somewhere between 6 B.C. and A.D. 3. The tale of his extraordinary birth in the city of Bethlehem in Judaea (the southern area of Palestine under Roman rule) is found in the Gospels of Matthew and Luke, but not in those of Mark and John. Other differences in these books about Jesus' childhood make it difficult to know what is true. There is some agreement, however, in these four books about the activities of his adult life.

Teachings Angered Religious Leaders

Jesus began his life as a preacher, teacher, and healer after his baptism by John the Baptist, a religious reformer. Wandering throughout Galilee, in the northern part of Palestine, Jesus taught the importance of having faith in God and of having love for mankind. Without this faith and love, he said, religious ceremonies, works of charity, and prayer were all worthless. Jesus also attacked the belief that Jews were the "chosen people" of God. He preached that all people could enter Heaven if they served God correctly. And Jesus expanded this idea of a brotherhood of all mankind by rejecting family relations, claiming instead that all men and all women were brothers and sisters under God. This type of teaching angered many Jewish religious leaders. They felt that Jesus disregarded, or ignored, many Jewish religious traditions. But Jesus challenged their power and beliefs by quoting stories from the Old Testament, which he knew very well, to emphasize a point he was making. Often they could not disagree.

The crucifixion of Jesus. Engraving by Lucas van Leyden, 1517.

Jesus preached through parables, stories about everyday life that help to explain difficult moral or religious principles. Through these stories, he attracted a large following. His supposed ability to perform miracles, on which all the Gospels agree, also drew many people to him. In his first miracle, recorded in the Gospel of John, Jesus changes water into wine at a wedding feast. As his story continues in each of the

Gospels, Jesus' miracles became greater. He walks on water, cures the lame and the blind, feeds 5,000 followers with five loaves of bread and two fishes, and raises the dead.

Disciples Spread His Message

Included in Jesus' large following was a special group of 12 disciples. Jesus gave them the task of spreading his teachings, first within Palestine, and later throughout the world. He taught them to pray and gave them powers of healing. But his attempts to teach them his message often failed. And he could not depend on them when he was in need. One of them, Judas Iscariot, betrayed Jesus to the Roman authorities for money by identifying him with a kiss. In doing so, Jesus was arrested and sentenced to death shortly thereafter. Another, Simon Peter, denied any knowledge of Jesus when he feared he might be arrested and killed by the Romans.

After preaching for almost three years in Galilee, Jesus went to Jerusalem in Judaea to celebrate the Jewish festival of Passover. When he arrived, he preached to cheering crowds. But Jewish religious leaders, afraid Jesus was becoming too powerful, had him arrested. Since Jesus claimed to be the Messiah, the expected king of the Jews, he was accused of blasphemy, or insulting God. Afterward, he was handed over to Pontius Pilate, the Roman ruler of Judaea. Pilate charged Jesus with sedition—the act of rebelling against Roman authority—since he claimed to be the leader of the Jewish people. Jesus was then put to death through crucifixion.

Historically, Jesus' life ended here. According to the Gospels, however, Jesus arose from his grave three days later, appeared to his disciples, and urged them to spread his message. He then rose into Heaven. His disciples, especially Paul and Peter, helped establish Christianity as a religion in the years after Jesus' death.

Jomo Kenyatta

First president of Kenya

Born October 20, 1891, Ichaweri, British East Africa

Died August 21, 1978, Mombasa, Kenya

"Under Kenyatta's guidance, Kenya prospered and became a model for other newly free African nations."

In 1895 England took control of the present-day country of Kenya, calling the area British East Africa. In the early 1900s, European settlers moved into the region, taking land away from the native peoples. By the 1920s, the area had been renamed Kenya Colony, and the white settlers dominated the government and owned most of the farmland in the country. The native Kenyans, denied land and power, soon organized to seek reform and independence. Jomo Kenyatta emerged as their leader. He not only helped bring about independence but was elected the first president of an independent Kenya. Under Kenyatta's guidance, Kenya prospered and became a model for other newly free African nations. To his people, he became known as *Mzee,* the "wise father" of Kenya.

According to most sources, Kenyatta was born on October 20, 1891, in the village of Ichaweri. His parents were Muigai, a farmer, and Wambui. He and his family were members of the Kikuyu, Kenya's largest ethnic group. His original name was Johnstone Kamau, but he later adopted the name

Kenyatta from the Kikuyu name for a workers' belt, *mucibi wa kinyata*, that he wore when he was young. While growing up, Kenyatta received five years of schooling at the Church of Scotland mission school near the capital city of Nairobi.

In the early 1920s, Kenyatta moved to Nairobi where he worked a series of minor jobs. Having grown up on a small farm, he knew firsthand the poor conditions under which native Kenyans lived. This inspired him to join the Kikuyu Central Association (KCA), a group that worked to improve the living conditions of the Kikuyu. In 1928 he became the association's general secretary. The following year he was chosen to edit the association's newsletter, *Muigwithania,* believed to be the first journal published by native Kenyans.

Travels to England to Seek Reforms

In 1930 Kenyatta traveled to England as a representative of the KCA. He lobbied the English government for land reform and for the development of independent Kikuyu schools. Only the schools were granted. Although he traveled throughout Europe, including the Soviet Union, he remained mostly in England for the next sixteen years. Kenyatta promoted native Kenyan causes by writing letters to government officials and articles for newspapers. In the mid-1930s, he studied anthropology at the London School of Economics and Political Science. He wrote a series of papers about Kikuyu culture, which were collected into a book and published in 1938 as *Facing Mount Kenya.* Highly praised by critics, the book is one of the first scholarly works about an African culture written by an African.

Kenyatta returned to Kenya in 1946. He was immediately elected president of the Kenyan African Union, a new political party. He spoke out for voting rights for native Kenyans and for the equal division of farmland between blacks and whites. His fiery speeches attracted crowds of native Kenyans and membership in the Kenyan African Union grew to over 100,000.

At this same time, a radical movement known as the Mau Mau arose in Kenya. Its members sought to rid the country of all white Europeans. In 1952 the Mau Mau killed a group of white settlers and blacks suspected of cooperating with the government. In October of that year, Kenyatta and five others were arrested and charged with being organizers of this movement. Although Kenyatta denied involvement, he was convicted the following April and sentenced to seven years of hard labor. He was released in 1959, but restricted to house arrest for two more years.

Prison Doesn't Weaken Kenyatta's Popularity

Kenyatta remained popular even during the time he was in prison. In 1960 a new political party, the Kenyan African National Union, elected him its president while he was still under house arrest. After his final release, Kenyatta negotiated with the English government for a new Kenyan constitution. England finally submitted to his demands and granted Kenya independence on December 12, 1963. Kenyatta was quickly elected the country's first president.

Kenyatta built his government on the slogan *Harambee*, Swahili for "let us all pull together." He ended all forms of discrimination between blacks and whites in the new country, giving native Kenyans positions on all levels of government. White settlers who sold vast areas of farmland to the blacks were encouraged to remain in Kenya to work in business, manufacturing, and tourism. Kenyatta spent a third of the national budget on education. All children received free primary education while older Kenyans received technical or on-the-job training. The economy prospered, allowing Kenyatta to spend more money on health and agriculture.

Kenyatta became a leader throughout eastern Africa, and other nations sought his advice. In 1971 he helped settle a border dispute between the neighboring countries of Uganda and Tanzania. Yet he was not so diplomatic at home, often censoring his political rivals. In 1974 he passed a decree outlawing all other political parties except his own. However, Kenyatta stabilized the government and brought peace and prosperity to Kenya, and even his rivals mourned his death in 1978.

Ruhollah Khomeini

Iranian religious leader

*Born November 2, c. 1902,
Khomein, Persia*

*Died June 3, 1989,
Tehran, Iran*

When he was 75 years old, Ruhollah Khomeini inspired a revolution that overthrew the Iranian government of Muhammad Reza Shah Pahlevi. Khomeini was the leading *ayatollah* (supreme religious leader) of Iran's Shiites, members of the second largest branch of Islam. Upon coming to power, he established in Iran an Islamic republic, a government based on the religious laws of Islam and run by Islamic clergy. He became the ultimate authority in the new government and called for religious revolutions in surrounding countries. He opposed Western ideas and approved of the seizure of the American embassy in the Iranian capital of Tehran, in what became known as the Iran hostage crisis. Feared and hated in the West, Khomeini was passionately supported by millions of Iranians.

Probably born in 1902, Khomeini was the fourth child of Sayyad Mostafa Musavi, a poor religious scholar, and Hajar. Upon his birth, his parents named him Ruhollah, meaning "the spirit of God." After his father's death in 1903, Khomeini was

"Feared and hated in the West, Khomeini was passionately supported by millions of Iranians."

raised by a relatively wealthy aunt since his mother was just a teenager. He was educated in a local Islamic school where he studied Arabic, logic, arithmetic, and the Qur'an, the Islamic holy book. In the early 1920s, Khomeini completed his religious education in the northwestern city of Qom, the most conservative religious center in Iran. In Qom he studied under Shiite scholars, concentrating on traditional Islamic law, ethics, and spiritual philosophy.

By the late 1920s, Khomeini had become a mullah, a Shiite priest. He gave lectures on ethics and philosophy and began to attract many students. At this time, Iran was under the control of a new ruler, Reza Shah Pahlevi. He sought to modernize the country, breaking Islamic traditions that had previously governed it. He abandoned the Islamic calendar and adopted the Western one. He further upset Muslims (followers of Islam) by banning traditional Islamic attire: beards and turbans for men and veils for women. Because religious leaders wielded great power in Iranian society, Reza Shah passed regulations limiting their power. Many mullahs, including Khomeini, were placed under house arrest.

In 1930 Khomeini married Batul bint Mirza Muhammad al-Saqafi, the ten-year-old daughter of a fellow religious leader. Over the next twenty years, he traveled throughout Iran, lecturing to students. Through his writings on Islamic law and ethics, Khomeini had advanced in the ranks of the Shiite clergy and had gathered a group of disciples. Sometime in the 1950s, he was recognized as an *ayatollah,* giving him the ability to rule on questions concerning Islamic law.

Muhammad Reza Shah Pahlevi, the son of Reza Shah, had succeeded his father in 1941. He not only continued his father's plans to modernize Iran but added to them as well. In 1961, with financial help from the United States, he began a reform program called the "White Revolution." Under this program, public education and construction increased, women gained more rights, and lands of the wealthy were divided among most of Iran's citizens. Shah Pahlevi also allowed non-Muslims to hold positions in the government for the first time.

Arrested After Criticizing Shah

In 1963, while speaking in Qom, Khomeini criticized Shah Pahlevi for reducing the role of Islam in Iranian society. Khomeini was immediately arrested, but then released when his followers started a riot. This episode confirmed Khomeini as the leading *ayatollah* and the chief opponent of the shah. The following year, after criticizing Shah Pahlevi even more, Khomeini was forced to leave the country. He settled in neighboring Iraq, where his visitors were watched by Iraqi and Iranian secret police.

When the price of oil (one of Iran's major exports) rose in the early 1970s, the country prospered. New buildings and factories were constructed. However, the new wealth was not divided equally among all Iranians, and those who remained poor began to revolt. Shah Pahlevi expanded SAVAK, his secret police, to brutally put down any rebellions against his government. His plan backfired as massive riots broke out and Iranians called for the return of Khomeini. Thousands of Iranians were killed in the uprisings.

Iraq expelled Khomeini in October 1978 for his persistent attacks on Shah Pahlevi. Khomeini traveled to France, where he continued to urge his followers to overthrow the Iranian government. Unable to control the country any longer, Shah Pahlevi finally fled on January 16, 1979. A month later, Khomeini arrived back in Iran, greeted by thousands of wild supporters. He established an Islamic republic in Iran, and hundreds of men, women, and children who were suspected of having supported the former shah were arrested and killed.

Supports Iran Hostage Crisis

On November 4, 1979, a small group of Iranian demonstrators, calling themselves "students," seized the United States Embassy in Tehran, eventually holding 52 Americans hostage. Knowing the United States had supported the shah, Khomeini refused to have the hostages released. Relations between the United States and the new government in Iran deteriorated as the Iran hostage crisis continued. On April 24, 1980, the United States attempted a rescue mission, but it failed and eight rescuers died. After 444 days in captivity, the hostages were finally released on January 20, 1981.

In September 1980, in a dispute over territory, Iraq had invaded Iran. Because the seizure of the U.S. embassy had been a violation of international law, many countries refused to help Iran. The Iraqis was successful at the beginning of the Iran-Iraq War, but by 1982 the Iranians had forced them to retreat. However, Khomeini said Iran would not stop the fighting until Iraqi president Saddam Hussein had been removed and Iraq had been turned into an Islamic republic. The continuing war brought new horrors to Iran: the Iraqis bombed Iranian cities and used poison gas on Iranian troops. Without needed supplies to continue the war, Iran was forced to accept a United Nations cease-fire agreement in 1988.

The last years of Khomeini's reign were unhappy. The eight-year war had destroyed Iran's economy, and many of Khomeini's fellow clergy in the government quarreled among themselves. One of Khomeini's last official acts was to sentence the English novelist Salman Rushdie to death for writing *The Satanic Verses,* which Khomeini believed was offensive to Islam. When Khomeini died on June 3, 1989, millions in Iran mourned his death. The succeeding government in Iran, however, softened many of his policies and relations with Western nations improved.

Lao-tzu

*Chinese philosopher,
supposed founder of Taoism*

Lived c. sixth century B.C.

Much of what is known about ancient China has been passed down through the centuries in the form of legends. It is often impossible to know what is true in them. Such is the case with the legend describing the life of the Chinese philosopher Lao-tzu. Historians cannot be sure whether he even existed. Nor can they be sure whether the moral philosophy credited to him, known as Taoism, was actually his. Regardless, the teachings associated with Lao-tzu, the *Tao Te Ching*, continue to shape the outlook of millions of people in eastern Asia and elsewhere.

Legend states that Lao-tzu was born in 604 B.C. in the village of Quren in the present-day province of Hunan in southeast China. He had been conceived 62 years earlier when his mother looked at a fiery meteor passing across the sky. After having spent so many years in the womb, he was already a white-haired old man when his mother gave birth to him while leaning against a plum tree. He immediately assumed the role

"The teachings associated with Lao-tzu, the Tao Te Ching, continue to shape the outlook of millions of people in eastern Asia and elsewhere."

of sage (wise man) and became known as Lao-tzu (Chinese for "old master" or "old philosopher").

Lao-tzu reportedly went to the capital city of Loyang. Here he served in the royal court of the Chou dynasty as a librarian or a historian in charge of sacred books. He married and had a son, Tsung. Many later generations, including the T'ang dynasty emperors (A.D. 618-907), claimed to be descendants of Tsung. During this time, Lao-tzu's fame as a sage spread throughout China. Many disciples came to him from all over the land. One of those who supposedly came to hear his words was Confucius (see **Confucius**), another Chinese sage. Whether these two actually met is questioned. However, sculptings on tombstones that still exist reportedly show the two men together.

Vanishes into the Mountains

How Lao-tzu disappeared is also legendary. Tired of taking part in everyday life, he left the royal court and rode westward on a water buffalo. Soon he came to the Hsien-ku Pass, where the border guard begged him to write down all of his wisdom. Pausing for only a brief time, Lao-tzu wrote a book of two sections of about 5,000 characters. In the book he explained his ideas concerning the *Tao* (Chinese for "way" or "path") and the *Te* (Chinese for "virtue" or "power"). This book thus became known as the *Lao-tzu* or, more commonly, the *Tao Te Ching*. After having written his last character, Lao-tzu wandered into the K'un-lun mountains in western China and was never seen again.

Many modern scholars argue that the *Tao Te Ching* cannot have been the work of one author. They believe it was written over the span of a few centuries, beginning in the sixth century B.C. Nonetheless, it has influenced art and thinking in eastern Asia for over 2,000 years.

Taoism Stresses Inaction

Tao is the natural order or course of the universe—it inhabits every created thing. To understand this natural order and to return to it, Lao-tzu believed women and men must follow the principle of *wu-wei* (Chinese for "no action"). This does not mean that people should shun every single action. The absence of movement would be totally unnatural. Instead, one should act spontaneously, instinctively. Any action that is extreme or aggressive should be avoided.

Lao-tzu insisted in the *Tao Te Ching* that people should not struggle to achieve their desires, but should aim for simplicity in all things. They should allow nature to flow over them the way water freely flows down a stream. Believing that goodness is a virtue, Lao-tzu also urged people to have a deep love of both the earth and their fellow man. Only when people act in this way will they come to understand the *Tao*. Once they do, he believed, they will have a long life of peace and harmony.

What is *Tao?*— From the *Tao Te Ching*

"Tao is empty (like a bowl).

It may be used but its capacity is never exhausted.

It is bottomless, perhaps the ancestor of all things.

It blunts its sharpness,

It unties its tangles,

It softens its light.

It becomes one with the dusty world.

Deep and still, it appears to exist forever."

Mao Zedong

Founder of the People's Republic of China

*Born December 26, 1893,
Shoashan, China*

*Died September 9, 1976,
Beijing, China*

"Mao's actions changed the lives of one-quarter of the people on this planet."

Mao Zedong is one of the greatest figures in China's four thousand-year history and one of the most important leaders of any country in the twentieth century. His actions changed the lives of one-quarter of the people on this planet. Born among China's peasants (poor farmers), he grew up in a country weakened by overpopulation and by a failing government. To empower the peasants and to restore the strength of China, he led a revolution. He was successful, and China prospered during the first few years of his new government. However, he soon tried to extend his government's control over the peasants, resulting in the worst famine in the history of the world. Civil wars and quarrels among government officials marked the remaining years of his leadership.

Mao was born in 1893 in the small village of Shaoshan in Hunan, a province in central China. Although his parents, Mao Jen-shen and Wen Qimei, were peasants, his family never lacked food or clothing. Mao began working in the fields around his home when he was five and did not begin school until he was seven. In 1910 he was sent to a more modern school in a nearby town. He studied traditional works of Chinese history and literature and modern works that offered solutions to China's current problems.

At this time, China was collapsing. For thousands of years, China had been controlled by dynasties, periods in which a particular family ruled, sometimes for centuries. Under the current dynasty, the Manchus or Ch'ing, foreigners invaded China, sparking civil wars. Chinese peasants suffered. In 1912 a revolution led by Sun Yat-sen overthrew the Manchus and a new government was formed. However, Sun could not unify the country and by 1916 power had fallen into the hands of military generals, or warlords, who controlled the numerous provinces in the country.

Learns from the Russian Revolution

While chaos reigned over China, Mao completed his education at a teacher's training college in Changsha, Hunan's capital city. Hoping to find a solution to China's crisis, he and other intellectuals began to look at the Communist government recently formed in Russia by Vladimir Lenin (see **Vladimir Lenin**). Lenin had shown that Russian workers could carry out a revolution and gain control of the government. Mao believed Chinese peasants could do the same. In 1921 he helped found the Chinese Communist party, which grew rapidly over the next few years.

In 1927 China came under the control of the Nationalist government led by Chiang Kai-shek (see **Chiang Kai-shek**). The Nationalists wanted to keep control of China in the hands of landowners and businessmen, but the Communists wanted the country turned over to the peasantry. In April 1927, fearing the influence of the Communists, Chiang turned his army against them, slaughtering thousands.

During the next seven years, Mao and other Communists hid in remote mountainous regions in southern China. They successfully built a strong rebel government in this area, attracting more and more people to their cause. After repeated attacks by Nationalist forces, the Communists began a 6,000-

mile journey to the north in 1934. During this "Long March," the Communists fought constant battles and suffered incredible hardships. By the time they reached their destination the following year, more than half of the original marchers had died. For his courage and leadership during this journey, Mao was elected chairman of the Chinese Communist party.

Creates a Communist Nation

A truce between the Communists and the Nationalist government was declared when Japan invaded China in 1937. During World War II (1939-45), the two sides fought uneasily against this common enemy. After the war, they resumed their battle against each other. By 1949 the Nationalist government had been driven from the country and Mao proclaimed the founding of the People's Republic of China.

Mao immediately ordered the peasants to seize property from the landlords who controlled almost all the farmland. Over the next few years, life improved for the peasants as they grew more than enough food to eat. In 1953 Mao directed that all farms be pooled into cooperatives, where numerous peasant families would work together on a larger tract of land. Within two years, almost two-thirds of all peasants had joined cooperatives. Farm output increased dramatically. Peasants sold the extra food they grew and many of them became prosperous.

Mao had a vision of an industrial China. To raise the money needed to build industries, Mao turned to the peasants. In 1956 he decreed that all farms, animals, and tools be placed under government control. Peasants were forced to work on what were called collective farms. The government dictated what would be grown, how much of it, and what the peasants would be paid for their work. Within months, all of China's six million peasants were working in collectives. They lost what little wealth they had.

That same year Mao encouraged people to offer helpful criticism of the Communist party, a policy he called "Let One Hundred Flowers Bloom." Party leaders, quickly attacked for being corrupt, convinced Mao to reject this policy. In 1957 Mao called those people who spoke out "enemies" or "rightists." Nearly one million people were condemned as rightists and sent to jail or prison camps during the next year.

The Great Leap Forward

To make China equal with industrial nations, Mao launched his Great Leap Forward program in 1958. With the promise of a better future, the government encouraged people to work day and night to increase production. In a drive to make steel, people melted all the tools they had, but their primitive methods produced useless steel. To win the favor of high government leaders, local party officials inflated farm output figures. The government took grain from the peasants based on these high, false amounts. As a result, the peasants were left with nothing, and they ate tree bark, grass roots, and earth. Between 1959 and 1961, 30 million peasants starved to death.

In the early 1960s, Mao stepped down as leader of the government, but still controlled the Chinese Communist party. The new leaders, more moderate, worked to rebuild the country. They relaxed government controls and China prospered over the next few years. In 1966, however, Mao attacked these leaders, saying they were betraying the radical ideas of the original revolution. He then called on young Chinese to rebel against party officials, starting the Cultural Revolution. Bands of young Chinese, called Red Guards, ransacked museums, libraries, temples, and people's homes. They captured and publicly beat millions of officials, intellectuals, and former landowners. At least 400,000 of these people were beaten to death.

In 1967 the Red Guards began to fight among themselves. By summer, with millions of workers and soldiers joining the battle, China was in turmoil. The following year Mao ordered the Red Guards to disband and peace was restored. Mao then regained authority in the government and worked to improve relations with other countries. A visit by United States president Richard Nixon in 1972 eventually led to diplomatic contact with the United States after decades of hostile relations. Mao's health declined in the next few years, and moderates and radicals in the government fought for control. When Mao died in September 1976, the new leaders began to steer China away from his strict policies.

Moses

Hebrew prophet

Born c. late thirteenth century B.C., Egypt

Died c. early eleventh century B.C., Mount Pisgah, present-day Jordan

"It is written that Moses led the Hebrew people out of slavery in Egypt and gave to them the laws that formed the basis of the Jewish religion."

The chief sources of information about Moses' life are the second through fifth books of the Old Testament of the Bible—Exodus, Leviticus, Numbers, and Deuteronomy. From these sources alone, he is considered to be one of the great figures in Hebrew history. It is written that Moses led the Hebrew people out of slavery in Egypt and gave to them the laws that formed the basis of the Jewish religion. He is also held as a prophet (one whose words are inspired by God) by Christians and Muslims.

As recounted in the Bible, Moses was born to Amram and Jochebed, a Hebrew couple enslaved in Egypt. To limit the growth of the slaves, the Egyptian pharaoh had ordered all newborn male Hebrews drowned in the Nile River. Determined to save Moses' life, Jochebed placed him in a basket when he was three months old. She then set the basket in the Nile where the pharaoh's daughter came to bathe. Upon finding the child, the princess adopted him as her own and raised him as an Egyptian.

After he had grown, Moses one day saw an Egyptian beating a Hebrew slave to death. He stepped in and killed the Egyptian. When the pharaoh found out, he tried to have his foster son executed. Moses then fled to Midian, an ancient region south of the present-day country of Jordan. Here he remained with the family of the Midianite priest Jethro, eventually marrying his daughter Zipporah.

Speaks Directly to God

Many years later, while tending his father-in-law's sheep, Moses came upon a bush that was burning but was not being consumed. Drawing closer, he heard God's voice speaking to him from the flames. God instructed Moses to return to Egypt and lead the Hebrews out of slavery.

On his way back to Egypt, Moses met his brother Aaron, who then became his assistant. After reaching Egypt, the two brothers tried to convince the pharaoh to release the Hebrews, but the pharaoh refused. In response, Moses delivered from God a series of ten plagues on Egypt, which included the waters of the Nile turning to blood and locusts swarming over the land. The tenth plague resulted in the death of all firstborn sons of the Egyptians. Only after this did the pharaoh finally agree to Moses' demands.

Over 600,000 Hebrews took part in the exodus from Egypt. They had not been gone very long, however, when the pharoah changed his mind and sent his troops to recapture them. Moses and his people reached the Red Sea before the Egyptians were upon them. According to the Bible, Moses raised his staff and parted the waters, and the Hebrews traveled safely across on dry land. When the Egyptians tried to follow, the waters closed and engulfed them.

Receives the Ten Commandments

Though free from the Egyptians, the Hebrews faced many difficulties as they roamed through the deserted lands of the present-day Sinai Peninsula. The constant lack of food and water and attacks by other tribes they met threatened Moses and his people. After three months of wandering, they came upon Mount Sinai in the southern part of the peninsula. While the people waited below, Moses climbed the mountain. It was here, the Bible states, that God gave Moses the Ten Commandments, a moral code the Hebrews were to live by. Among the acts the code forbade were murder, adultery, and stealing.

Most laws at that time had been established only to keep order in society. They were written by rulers, who themselves were above the very laws they set down. The laws of the Ten Commandments differed in that they affected everyone equally. The code applied not only to social affairs but to religious ones as well. The religious laws of Judaism, Christianity, and Islam are based on the principles of this code.

Led by Moses, the Hebrews wandered for forty years in the wilderness of the Sinai Peninsula. During this time, Moses developed the Hebrew system of worship. He had to face many more battles with tribes whose lands the Hebrews crossed, and he also had to calm many rebellions by his people. Finally, they reached the Jordan River, which separated them from their destination of Canaan (roughly the present-day country of Israel). Moses saw this land from Mount Pisgah in present-day northeast Jordan, but never entered Canaan as he died there on the mountain. According to the Bible, Moses was 120 years old at his death.

Muhammad

Founder of Islam

Born c. 570,
Mecca, present-day Saudi Arabia

Died 632,
Medina, present-day Saudi Arabia

B efore the seventh century, Arabia (peninsula mainly occupied by the present-day country of Saudi Arabia) was a wild desert land populated by wandering tribes. These people fought bloody battles among themselves, raiding each other's flocks and women. They mostly worshiped nature gods and spirits that lived in trees, springs, and stones. Around 610 a man named Muhammad began to spread a religion that would eventually unite the people in this region. He preached a belief in one God who created the world and who sat in judgment over it. He instructed people to submit to the will of God. Hence, the religion he founded came to be known as *Islam* (submission) and a follower of that religion a *Muslim* (one who submits). Muslims believe Muhammad was God's last prophet, following the earlier Christian prophets Abraham, Moses (see **Moses**), and Jesus (see **Jesus**).

Muhammad was born around 570 in the city of Mecca in present-day Saudi Arabia. He was a member of the Hashim clan of the mighty Quraysh tribe. His father, Abd Allah, died

"Muslims believe Muhammad was God's last prophet, following the earlier Christian prophets Abraham, Moses, and Jesus."

shortly before his birth. His mother, Amina, died when he was six years old. After living with his grandfather for two years, Muhammad joined the family of his uncle, Abu Talib, the new leader of the Hashim. While living with his uncle, Muhammad tended sheep and went on caravans (trading expeditions) across the desert to Syria.

When Muhammad was about 25, he began working for Khadija, a wealthy widow involved in the caravan trade. Although she was 15 years older than he was, he soon married her. They had two sons, both of whom died young, and four daughters. Their marriage was happy and prosperous, and Muhammad became a respected merchant in Mecca.

Receives God's Message from the Angel Gabriel

Around the age of 40, Muhammad began to spend time meditating in a cave on Mount Hira outside Mecca. According to Muslims, he had a vision of the angel Gabriel who told him to spread the message of God to his people. Muhammad did not believe this vision at first, thinking instead he had been possessed by evil spirits. When he described his vision to Khadija, however, she immediately believed it was true, saying he was a prophet (one whose words are inspired by God). More visions and revelations soon came to Muhammad and he began to preach what he was told in the visions. The messages he received and the speeches he made were later written down to form the Islamic holy book, the Qur'an.

The message Muhammad passed on to his people was simple: there was only one God (known to Muslims as Allah) who had created the universe and who now governed it. Muhammad was God's messenger sent to spread God's laws and to warn people of the punishments if they disobeyed those laws. At first Muhammad gathered only a few followers. Most Meccans were outraged by his attacks on their lifestyle and on the pagan gods they worshiped in Mecca's sacred temple, the Kaaba. In 622, because of rising hostility, Muhammad and about 70 Muslims fled to the city of Medina (then known as Yathrib), 250 miles north of Mecca. This flight is called the Hegira and marks the beginning of the Muslim calendar. The people of Medina welcomed Muhammad and accepted his teachings.

Sets Down the Five Pillars of Islam

In Medina Muhammad became not only a religious leader but a political one as well. According to Muslim tradition, the messages Muhammad received at this time decreed how Muslims were to live. He made these divine rules into laws. He abolished the worship of other gods, regulated the practice of slavery, restricted divorce, and banned war or violence except in defense of God, an act called *jihad*. Drinking alcohol and eating pork were also forbidden. Muhammad dictated five duties Muslims had to follow, called the Five Pillars of Islam: Muslims must accept God and Muhammad as his messenger; they must pray five times a day to God; they must give money to the poor; they must fast between sunrise and sunset during Ramadan, the ninth month of the Muslim year; and they must make a pilgrimage (called a *hajj*) at least once during their lives to pray in Mecca.

At first, the Muslims faced Jerusalem when they prayed, like the Jews. However, the Jews in Medina refused to recognize Muhammad as a prophet and soon plotted with his enemies in Mecca. Muhammad angrily drove them from Medina and ordered the Muslims to face Mecca when praying. To weaken his enemies in Mecca, Muhammad began raiding caravans traveling to that city in 624. The Meccans immediately declared war. After a series of indecisive battles, the Muslims successfully defended Medina from a siege of 10,000 Meccans in 627. A great number of tribes in the region soon converted to Islam, recognizing Muhammad as a prophet and leader. Finally, in 628 the Meccans agreed to sign a treaty ending hostilities.

Muhammad and the Muslims in Medina marched to Mecca in 630. They met little opposition upon entering the city, and Muhammad forgave all those who accepted him as a prophet of God. He smashed all the pagan idols in the Kaaba and turned it into a mosque, an Islamic house of worship. Most tribes in Arabia were now united by the Islamic faith and Muhammad was the most powerful leader in that region. From

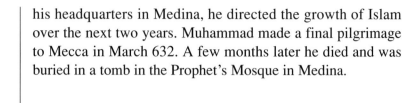

his headquarters in Medina, he directed the growth of Islam over the next two years. Muhammad made a final pilgrimage to Mecca in March 632. A few months later he died and was buried in a tomb in the Prophet's Mosque in Medina.

Gamal Abdal Nasser

First elected president of Egypt

Born January 15, 1918,
Alexandria, Egypt

Died September 28, 1970,
Cairo, Egypt

Beginning in 525 B.C. and continuing for the next 2,000 years, Egypt came under the control of numerous foreign powers. The first of these was the Persian Empire. A succession of conquerors followed, including Alexander the Great (see **Alexander the Great**) in 332 B.C., Muslim Arabs in 642, and the Ottoman Empire in 1517. In the late nineteenth century, while under the domination of England, the Arabic people of Egypt began their final struggle for freedom. A leader in the Egyptian nationalist (independence) movement was Gamal Abdal Nasser. He dreamed of creating not only an independent Egypt but a unified Arab state stretching from Egypt throughout southwest Asia. Only half of his dream came true.

Born in 1918, Nasser was the son of Abdul Nasser Hussein, a post office official, and Fahima. Just a few years after his birth, Nasser was sent to the Egyptian capital of Cairo to live with his unmarried uncle, Khalil Hussein. During the 1920s and 1930s, the nationalist movement gained strength. A

"Nasser dreamed of creating not only an independent Egypt but a unified Arab state stretching from Egypt throughout southwest Asia."

new constitution in 1923 had restored King Faud I to the Egyptian throne, but England still kept a tight hold on his powers. Nationalists rebelled against this continued English control of the Egyptian government. Cairo was a leading site of their activities.

Nasser joined the nationalist movement at a young age, taking an active role in student demonstrations. While involved in an anti-English protest in high school in 1935, he was shot and wounded by police. School officials then expelled him. Allowed to return a short time later, Nasser completed his education in 1937. He enrolled in law school that year, but dropped out after only a few months to attend the Royal Military Academy. While at the academy, he met fellow cadets who shared his strong nationalist feelings. The group of friends Nasser formed would eventually take over the government.

Creates Secret Organization to Gain Independence

Nasser was appointed an instructor at the Royal Military Academy in 1942. With his group of friends, he secretly formed the Society of Free Officers, an organization dedicated to freeing Egypt from English rule. This society and the nationalist movement received a boost when the first Arab-Israeli War erupted in 1948. In May of that year, England had given up control of Palestine, and Jews in the area established the nation of Israel (see **David Ben-Gurion**). Arab states immediately banded together to fight against Israeli independence.

The war went poorly for the Arabs and they were forced to sign a truce in 1949 recognizing the borders of Israel. Nasser and others held Egyptian rulers responsible for the Arab defeat and worked even harder to take over the government. In 1950 Nasser was secretly elected head of the Society of Free Officers. Two years later, with the nationalist movement reaching its peak, the Free Officers seized control of the government, overthrowing King Farouk, the son of Faud I. To run Egypt, Nasser established the Revolutionary Command Committee, a group of 11 military officers led by Nasser.

In 1953 the committee named General Muhammad Naguib as president and prime minister of Egypt. However, his cautious approach to governing the country upset the committee and in 1954 he was removed. Nasser was named the new prime minister. In 1956 he drafted a constitution that made Egypt a republic with one official political party. Islam became the state religion. In elections held in June of that year, Nasser was chosen the first president of the republic of Egypt.

To modernize Egypt and increase its economy, Nasser sought to build the Aswan High Dam near the city of Aswan on the Nile River. The completed dam would provide electric power as well as irrigation to a large section of Egypt. The United States and England agreed to lend money to build the dam, but withdrew the offer when they found out Egypt was receiving military arms from Communist countries. In response, Nasser seized the Suez Canal, the waterway along the upper northeast coast of Egypt connecting the Mediterranean Sea with the Red Sea. He planned to use the tolls collected from users of the canal to build his dam. England and France, which had controlled the canal, joined with Israel to attack Egypt in October 1956. Most countries around the world condemned the attack, and the United Nations stepped in to end the conflict in November.

Becomes a Leader Among Arabs

For standing up against these Western powers, Nasser was viewed as a heroic leader by other Arab nations. His dream of a unified Arab state began in 1958 when Syria asked to merge with Egypt. The combined countries formed the United Arab Republic, with Nasser as its president. He hoped other Arab nations would soon join this state, but his hopes were futile. In 1961 Syrian army officers gained control of that country and removed it from the Republic.

Nasser suffered his greatest defeat in 1967. Continuing disputes between Arab countries and Israel led Nasser to set up a blockade of Israel's only port in the Gulf of Aquaba (located at the northeast end of the Red Sea). On June 5, 1967, Israel launched a massive air attack that crippled Egypt, and by June 10 the war was over. Nasser resigned as president after Egypt's defeat in this Six-Day War, but the Egyptian people quickly convinced him to return to office.

During his time as president, Nasser helped modernize Egypt. He introduced land reforms that divided the estates of large landowners among poor farmers. He created more industries, raising the average living standard in the nation. He also brought more Egyptians into all levels of the government, replacing foreigners who had dominated those positions for so long. The Aswan High Dam, the greatest achievement of his government, was finally completed in 1970. Nasser died unexpectedly of a heart attack that same year.

Jawaharlal Nehru

First prime minister of independent India

Born November 14, 1889,
Allahabad, India

Died May 27, 1964,
India

At the beginning of the twentieth century, India had been under English control for almost 150 years. Seeking independence, many Indians had begun to rebel, sometimes violently. In this poor and oppressed country, Jawaharlal Nehru grew up in elegance and freedom. For the first third of his life, he did not experience the harsh measures of English rule. However, when he saw firsthand the miserable conditions of his fellow Indians, he realized his responsibility to help change their lives. He became a leader in the fight for independence. When the fight had been won, he assumed responsibility again. As India's first prime minister, Nehru bravely led the troubled country through its initial years of independence.

Nehru was born in the northern Indian city of Allahabad in 1889. His father, Motilal Nehru, was a distinguished and prosperous lawyer. Compared to those of other Indians, the Nehru home was a palace—swimming pools, horse stables, servants, and an extensive library. Nehru's early education came at home from English tutors. When he was 16, he trav-

"As India's first prime minister, Nehru bravely led the troubled country through its initial years of independence."

eled to England to complete his studies. He received a degree in natural science from Trinity College at Cambridge University, and then went on to study law at the Inner Temple in London. While in England, Nehru was more concerned with his studies than with Indian politics. When he returned to India as a lawyer in 1912, he took little part in public affairs. The highlight of this period was his 1916 marriage to Kamala Kaul.

Massacre and Poverty Grab Nehru's Attention

Two events prompted Nehru's entrance into the independence movement. In 1919 England enacted several bills restricting Indian civil rights. In response, many Indians rioted. In the city of Amritsar, an Indian mob burned banks and railroad stations. The following day, government troops fired upon an unarmed Indian crowd in the city, killing 400 and wounding 1,200. The following year, Nehru and his wife spent several months in a number of peasant villages, seeing for the first time the miserable conditions under which most Indians lived. Witnessing these events led Nehru to join the passive resistance (nonviolent) campaign for independence led by Mohandas Gandhi (see **Mohandas Gandhi**).

Nehru remained a part of the independence movement for the next 27 years. Because of his protest activities, he spent 10 of those years in jail. After release from his first jailing in 1922, he joined the Indian National Congress, a political party led by Gandhi. Two years later, he became general secretary of the party. Over the next decade, Nehru and Gandhi began to differ in their approach to independence. While Gandhi thought India could gain independence and still be part of the English empire, Nehru thought India should break away completely from England.

In 1929 Nehru became leader of the radical wing of the Indian National Congress. His passionate support of passive resistance (hunger strikes, mass demonstrations, marches), angered the English government, which considered him one of the most dangerous political rebels in India. Between 1931 and 1935, Nehru spent all but 10 months in jail. He was released in

1935 only because of his wife's poor health. She died of tuberculosis the following year. After her death, he became even more dedicated to India's independence movement.

The beginning of World War II in 1939 caused a shift in Nehru's approach toward England. He defended England's claim that it would grant India independence in exchange for India's support of its war effort. But other members of the

President Dwight Eisenhower greets Jawaharlal Nehru at the White House in 1956.

Indian National Congress, especially Gandhi, dismissed England's promise. Even though he was one of England's strongest supporters in the early stages of the war, Nehru was arrested in 1942 along with all Congress leaders. He was not released until June of 1945.

Agrees to the Creation of Pakistan

When the war ended in 1945, India was torn apart by religious differences. Muslims (followers of the religion of Islam) were the minority in India. They believed the Hindus (followers of the religion of Hinduism) would take over India after independence was granted and persecute them. Muslims demanded that the separate nation of Pakistan be created for them out of Indian soil. Nehru, now leader of the Indian National Congress, tried to keep the two sides united. Rising violence between Muslims and Hindus, however, convinced him to support the split between India and Pakistan.

When India was finally granted independence in August of 1947, Nehru was appointed its first prime minister. The migration of Muslims from India and Hindus from Pakistan caused further bloodshed until 1950. After securing a troubled peace in India, Nehru established five-year plans to tackle the social problems of poverty, starvation, disease, and illiteracy in his country. His first plan aimed at developing farms while the second plan, begun in 1956, focused on the development of industries.

In foreign affairs, Nehru pursued a neutral course, remaining friendly with both Communist and Western nations. To encourage peace in Asia, Nehru organized many conferences between representatives from Asian countries. He even extended these Asian relations to African countries. India's relationship with China, however, was not so calm. The two countries disagreed over the placement of borders in northern India. Discussions to settle the dispute proved useless, and in 1962 Chinese troops invaded the border region. The Indians, greatly outnumbered, surrendered the territory China claimed. An uneasy peace still existed between the two countries when Nehru died of a stroke in 1964. His daughter, Indira Gandhi, became India's prime minister two years later.

Julius K. Nyerere

First president of the United Republic of Tanzania

Born March 1922, Butiama, Tanganyika

During the nineteenth century, European explorers journeyed throughout Africa, claiming lands for their governments as they went along. In 1880 Germany took control of the area in east-central Africa that makes up present-day Tanzania. Zanzibar, an island off the east coast of this area, came under English rule ten years later. After Germany's defeat in World War I (1914-18), England took over Germany's land in Africa, naming it Tanganyika. In 1946 the United Nations directed England to set up a government in the country, but the Tanganyikans wanted complete independence and their own government. Julius K. Nyerere led this independence movement and brought freedom to Tanganyika in 1961. Two years later, he combined Tanganyika with Zanzibar to form the United Republic of Tanzania. While governing Tanzania, he became a leading figure in the drive for African unity.

Nyerere was born in 1922 in the northern Tanganyika village of Butiama. He was the son of Chief Burito Nyerere of the Zanaki tribe (the smallest of Tanganyika's 113 tribes) and

"While governing Tanzania, Nyerere became a leading figure in the drive for African unity."

Mugaya, one of Burito's 22 wives. After spending his early years tending his father's goats, Nyerere was finally allowed to attend a boarding school when he 12. Because of his high intelligence, he was accepted a few years later into Tanganyika's only secondary school, run by Roman Catholic missionaries (teachers who try to convert others to different religious beliefs).

After graduating in 1943, Nyerere entered Makerere College, a teacher's college in the neighboring country of Uganda. Upon receiving his diploma in 1945, he taught in a Roman Catholic school in the Tanganyika city of Tabora. In 1949 he was awarded a government scholarship to attend Edinburgh University in Scotland, becoming the first Tanganyikan to study at a university in the United Kingdom. He graduated with a master's degree in history and economics in 1952 and returned to teach in Tanganyika. The following year he married Maria Gabriel Magige, with whom he eventually had seven children.

Trades Teaching for Politics

At this time, England was in the process of forming a government that represented the Europeans and the Tanganyikans in the country equally. The Tanganyikans, who were the vast majority, did not want this unfair government and began pushing for complete independence. Nyerere quickly became involved in the movement. In 1953 he helped form the Tanganyika African National Union (TANU). Led by Nyerere, TANU sought independence through peaceful change. Having abandoned teaching for politics, Nyerere traveled to New York City in 1955 to address the United Nations on the issue of Tanganyikan independence. His appearance there established him as the country's leading spokesman.

In 1958 and again in 1960, Nyerere was elected to the Tanganyikan Legislative Council, the ruling body under the English governor. When Tanganyika was finally granted independence in 1961, Nyerere became prime minister. The following year, after the country was declared to be a republic, Nyerere was elected Tanganyika's first president. Zanzibar, which gained its independence from England in 1963, then joined with Tanganyika in April 1964 to form the United Republic of Tanzania.

On April 22, 1964, President Julius Nyerere (seated left) and President Aseid Karume signed an agreement uniting Tanganyika and Zanzibar to create the Republic of Tanzania.

Beginning in 1965, Nyerere was elected to four five-year terms as president of Tanzania. He put the country on a socialist economic system based on the principle of *ujamaa* (Swahili for "familyhood"). The government took control of many businesses and industries. To increase agricultural production, Nyerere combined small farms into larger units called *ujamaa villages*. The government spent an equal amount of money on the development of rural areas as it did on cities. Seeking to have Tanzania advance by itself without the aid of foreign countries, Nyerere established free education throughout the country. Because of his program, Tanzania's literacy rate became the highest among African nations.

Seeks Cooperation and Unity in Africa

Nyerere was a key figure in African affairs. In 1963 he had helped found the Organization of African Unity, which promoted educational, scientific, and political cooperation among its member nations. He worked toward racial harmony in Africa and opposed the racist white governments of Namibia, Rhodesia (present-day Zimbabwe), and South Africa. In 1967 he formed a trading association with Kenya and Uganda called the East African Community.

However, this association fell apart after only ten years because of growing tensions between Nyerere and Ugandan dictator Idi Amin, who had come to power in 1971. During his reign, Amin murdered an estimated 200,000 Ugandans who opposed his brutal policies. In 1978, Amin's army seized territory just inside the border of Tanzania. Nyerere responded the following year by sending Tanzanian troops into Uganda to help Ugandans successfully overthrow Amin.

The costly war against Uganda and decreased trade in the early 1980s hurt the Tanzanian economy, forcing Nyerere to relax his government's control over businesses. Through his leadership, however, the government remained stable and the economy began to recover slowly in some areas. In 1985 Nyerere stepped down as president, but stayed on as chairman of the nation's sole political party, the Chama Cha Mapinduzi. Even after he retired from the party in 1990, Nyerere continued to influence on the politics in Tanzania.

Osman I

Founder of the Ottoman Empire
Born 1259
Died 1326

I n the middle of the thirteenth century, two great empires in eastern Asia were declining. The Byzantine Empire (the successor state to the old Roman Empire) could no longer protect its outer reaches. In 1204, the Byzantine capital of Constantinople (present-day Istanbul, Turkey) had fallen to Christian European warriors leading the Fourth Crusade. The empire of the Seljuks (Muslim Turks) lay directly east of the Byzantine Empire. It covered the eastern half of Asia Minor (a peninsula forming most of present-day Turkey) and parts of the present-day countries of Syria, Iraq, and Iran. This empire lost its independence in 1243 when Mongols, invading from the east, took control of the government.

Between these two wavering empires lived a group of Turkish nomads (wanderers) related to the Seljuks. One of their leaders was Ertogrul. He had been granted a parcel of land on the western border of the Seljuk Empire by one of its sultans (rulers) for helping in a battle against the Mongols. His job was to protect the Muslim Seljuk Empire against the

"Osman's conquests laid the foundation for the Ottoman Empire, one of the largest and longest-lived empires in history."

Christian forces controlling the Byzantine Empire. Although these empires were crumbling around him, Ertogrul remained committed to his job. He did not try to conquer territory beyond the land given him, but his son, Osman, did. From the time he assumed control of his father's land, he led a campaign to conquer the surrounding countryside. He carved out a state independent of either Byzantine or Mongol control. Osman's conquests laid the foundation for the Ottoman Empire, one of the largest and longest-lived empires in history.

Dreams of an Empire

Osman (also known as Othman) was born in 1259 in present-day Turkey. Few personal details exist about his life. One legend states that as a young man, he fell in love with Malkhatun and asked her to marry him. However, her father, a renowned holy man, refused. After several years of unhappiness, Osman had a dream in which a full moon sank into his chest. Out of his chest sprang a great tree, which grew to cover a world of gleaming cities and ripe pastures. Then a strong wind blew, pointing all the leaves of the tree toward the city of Constantinople in the distance. Malkhatun's father thought this dream meant that a union between Osman and his daughter would produce a great empire. He quickly changed his mind and agreed to their marriage.

Osman did, indeed, go on to create an empire. He assumed command of his father's land in 1288 and immediately began to extend its boundaries by conquering neighboring villages. In 1290 he declared that his area no longer came under the influence of the Seljuk Empire. When the Mongols had gained control of the empire, all Seljuk leaders were required to pay a yearly tribute (taxes) to the Mongols. In 1299 Osman stopped paying these tributes, and the Mongols did not bother him.

To help in his conquest of Byzantine areas, Osman recruited *ghazis,* nomad Muslim warriors devoted to the battle against Christian-held territories. Beginning in 1300 Osman and his warriors attacked and captured key Byzantine forts and cities, including Eskishehr, Inonu, Bilicik, and Yenishehr. By 1308 Osman had control over areas as far west as the Sakarya

River and the Sea of Marmara (on the west coast of present-day Turkey).

Attacks City of Bursa for Eighteen Years

The city of Bursa, however, remained out of Osman's grasp. An important Byzantine center at the foot of Mount Olympus (in present-day northwest Turkey), Bursa was strongly fortified. A high wall and several small forts surrounded the city. Even though Osman occupied all the land around Bursa, the city was still able to receive supplies from the neighboring port of Mudanya. Since he could not take the city by force, Osman set up a military blockade to force Bursa to surrender. The city repelled his repeated attacks and worked around his blockade for years. Finally, in 1321, Osman captured Mudanya, isolating Bursa from the outside world. Incredibly, the city refused to surrender for another five years. Then on April 6, 1326, Bursa fell and Osman's troops entered the city.

The surrender of Bursa marked a turning point in Osman's quest for power. Although he had been conquering areas since 1288, most of what he controlled was rural land. Bursa was a major commercial center open to the rest of the world and Osman made it the capital city of his ever-growing state. Shortly after the capture of Bursa, however, Osman died. He was buried in Bursa in a beautiful mausoleum that stood for centuries. His son, Orkhan, continued to expand the new state into Byzantine territory. This state, which came to be known as the Ottoman Empire, was ruled by Osman's descendants for almost six centuries.

Ptolemy I Soter

King of Egypt

*Born 367 B.C.,
Macedon*

*Died 285 B.C.,
Egypt*

*"Had Ptolemy not
spread Greek culture
throughout Egypt, the
history of Western
civilization (and our
modern world) would
have been permanently
changed."*

A general in the army of Alexander the Great (see **Alexander the Great**), Ptolemy I Soter became governor of Egypt after Alexander's death in 323 B.C. Through his vast empire, from Egypt east to India, Alexander had spread Hellenism, the culture and ideas of ancient Greece. Ptolemy remained loyal to Alexander's ideal. He became a founder of the Hellenistic civilization, the blending of Hellenism with other cultures in the areas surrounding the Mediterranean Sea and western Asia after Alexander's death. Had he not spread Greek culture throughout Egypt, the history of Western civilization (and our modern world) would have been permanently changed. For his achievements, Ptolemy is considered one of the most important rulers in world history.

Almost nothing is known about Ptolemy's early years. He was born in 367 B.C. in the ancient kingdom of Macedon (present-day country of Macedonia) to Lagus, a nobleman, and his wife, Arsinoe. One story claims that the Macedonian king Philip II, the father of Alexander, was actually the father of

Ptolemy. Whether this is true, Ptolemy and Alexander became close friends while both were still boys. When Alexander became king in 336 B.C., he made Ptolemy a member of his personal bodyguard. Alexander built his empire over the next 13 years, with Ptolemy serving him as a courageous general.

Brings Alexander's Body to Alexandria

Upon Alexander's death from a fever in 323 B.C., his empire was divided among his administrators and generals, a group known as the *Diadochi* (Greek for "successors"). Ptolemy received the governorship of Egypt. One of his first actions as governor was to obtain the body of Alexander, which he brought to the Egyptian capital city of Alexandria. He placed it in a gold coffin housed in a magnificent tomb. This act greatly enhanced Ptolemy's standing among the people of Alexandria, a city founded by Alexander.

Ptolemy's ability as a ruler, however, made him popular with all the people of Egypt. Among the *Diadochi,* he was the best administrator. He recognized the role the pharaoh had played in Egyptian life. Wisely, he did not establish himself as a Greek king but as a successor to the pharaohs of ancient Egypt. He kept many of the customs and traditions of Egypt's age-old civilization and he ruled carefully and compassionately.

At the same time, Ptolemy was committed to Alexander's dream of spreading Hellenism. Alexandria quickly became a center for the development of the Hellenistic civilization. In less than a hundred years, it rose to be the largest city the world had ever seen, measuring about four miles across and fifteen miles around. Three-quarters of a million people lived there. Ptolemy developed a constitution for Alexandria, which provided for a governing assembly that was served by a council. He also gave the city a law code based on Greek models.

Dedicated to Learning and the Arts

Ptolemy attracted to Alexandria many Greek scholars, poets, scientists, and philosophers who introduced Hellenism throughout Egypt. Included in this group were the philosopher

Demetrius Phalereus and the poet Callimachus. Ptolemy himself was something of a scholar. He wrote a *Life of Alexander,* a biography of the great leader that was highly regarded during that time. Perhaps the greatest of his Hellenistic achievements were the founding of a museum and a library in Alexandria. The museum functioned like a university, the first the ancient world had ever known. Historical records indicate that literature, science, grammar, geography, and philosophy were taught there. The library, probably a part of the museum, eventually housed almost a million volumes. Both the museum and the library lasted for centuries.

Fights for Control

After the death of Alexander, the regions along the eastern Mediterranean fell into turmoil. Many of the *Diadochi* fought among themselves for greater control in the area. In 319 B.C., to strengthen his position in Egypt, Ptolemy married Eurydice, the daughter of Antipater, a Macedonian general who worked to keep the empire together. A few years earlier, Ptolemy had seized control of Syria and Cyrenaica (eastern part of present-day Libya). In 315 B.C., Antigonus, who ruled Asia Minor (peninsula forming most of present-day Turkey), seized Syria. Over the next ten years, battles continued as the former generals under Alexander swapped lands. In 305 B.C., Ptolemy protected the people of Rhodes (a Greek island off the southwest coast of Turkey) against an attack by Antigonus's son, Demetrius. Grateful, the Rhodians gave Ptolemy the title *Soter,* meaning savior, by which he was known ever after.

That same year, Ptolemy declared himself king of Egypt. The battles between the *Diadochi* continued for some years, but Ptolemy's claim to Egypt's throne was secure. Although he had two sons by his wife Eurydice, he decided not to pass his throne to either of them. Instead, he chose Ptolemy Philadelphus, his son by his fourth wife, Berenice. In 285 B.C. Ptolemy retired and placed Philadelphus on the throne. He died shortly afterward. The dynasty founded by Ptolemy ruled Egypt for almost the next three hundred years. The famous Cleopatra (see **Cleopatra VII**) was the last ruler in the Ptolemaic dynasty.

Qin Shi Huang-di

Emperor of the Qin (Ch'in) dynasty who unified China

Born 259 B.C.

Died 210 B.C.

Beginning around 800 B.C., the country of China was torn apart by rival states or kingdoms battling for control of lands. By 400 B.C., only seven major kingdoms remained. These kingdoms continued fighting for the next two hundred years until the kingdom of Qin (Ch'in) gradually became the strongest. The king of Qin, later known as Qin Shi Huang-di (Ch'in Shih Hwang-ti), defeated all the remaining regional kings by 221 B.C. He then unified the country into an empire, ending six centuries of war. Although he ruled harshly, Qin Shi Huang-di created a centralized government in China that lasted for over 2,000 years.

Qin Shi Huang was born Ying Zheng in 259 B.C. to King Zhuang Xiang of Qin. When he was 13 years old, his father died. He assumed the throne of Qin and became known as King Zheng. He could not legally rule Qin by himself until he reached the age of 22, so his father's prime minister ruled with him. In 237 B.C., when King Zheng was ready to rule alone,

"Although he ruled harshly, Qin Shi Huang-di created a centralized government in China that lasted for over 2,000 years."

the prime minister and others plotted to take over the throne. King Zheng discovered the plot, however, and arrested them.

King Zheng then appointed the scholar Li Si as his major advisor. Together the two men planned the conquest of the other warring kingdoms in the country: Han, Zhao (Chao), Wei, Chu, Yan (Yen), and Qi (Ch'i). King Zheng began his mission in 230 B.C. by conquering Han, the weakest kingdom. Two years later, he captured Zhao. In 227 B.C., hoping to prevent an attack by King Zheng, the crown prince of Yan sent an assassin to kill him. After the plan failed, the king of Yan killed the crown prince to make peace. By 221 B.C., King Zheng had defeated the rest of the major kingdoms. He now ruled supreme over the country that came to bear the name of his kingdom: China (for Qin or Ch'in). Adopting the title of Shi Huang-di (first emperor), he became Qin Shi Huang-di, or the first emperor of the Qin dynasty.

Enacts Strict Reforms to Control China

Qin Shi Huang began his rule with a series of administrative reforms. He divided the country into 36 districts (*Jun*), each of which contained a number of counties (*Xian*). In each of the counties, there were a number of towns (*Xiang*). As emperor, Qin Shi Huang appointed all the officials in the districts and counties. Most of the officials were military officers who had served in battle under Qin Shi Huang. Through this system, the emperor was assured of strong support for his central government.

To prevent any rebellions by civilians, Qin Shi Huang ordered all private weapons to be turned in. He had the weapons melted down to form 12 bronze statues, each weighing 120 tons. They were placed in the front hall of his new palace in the capital city of Xian Yang. Qin Shi Huang then ordered 120,000 of the most powerful families in the country to move to Xian Yang so he could watch over them more easily. Those people who were considered rebellious or dangerous were moved far away from the areas of power.

To tighten his control over the country, Qin Shi Huang unified the code of laws. He developed laws describing the duties of government officials and the punishments if they neglected those duties. Punishments for criminal offenses were extremely harsh. A man caught stealing had his left foot cut off or his face branded. If a man committed a severe crime, he was torn apart by a chariot or his entire family was executed. Qin Shi Huang also unified measuring systems, currency, and written languages that had differed in the former kingdoms of China.

Builds Great Highways and the Great Wall

Qin Shi Huang undertook many large construction projects during his reign. One of these was the building of three imperial highways, known as *Chi Dao*. These highways were 300 feet wide, with pine trees planted along the sides every 30 feet. From Xian Yang, the completed highways stretched out 4,200 miles over China. Portions of *Chi Dao* remain today. Another project was the beginning of the world-famous Great Wall. To prevent invasions from northern countries, Qin Shi Huang had workers repair and link the old defensive walls built by the former kingdoms of Qin, Zhao, and Yan. From east to west, the wall extended over 1,400 miles. Tens of thousands of people were sent to build the wall, many of them prisoners. More than half died because of the harsh living conditions and the heavy labor.

Qin Shi Huang was especially cruel to scholars and philosophers who questioned his rule. In 213 B.C. he ordered the burning of almost all books in China. Only those books on medicine, on tree planting, and on religion were to be saved. Anyone who did not burn banned books was sent to work on the Great Wall for four years. Those people who openly spoke about banned books were executed. The following year, the emperor learned that a group of 460 Confucius scholars had talked among themselves, criticizing his government. After Qin Shi Huang ordered a full investigation, he sentenced them all to be buried alive in the capital.

In 210 B.C., while making his fifth inspection tour of China, Qin Shi Huang became ill and died. His body was carried back to his tomb in Xian Yang. His many mistresses and the artisans who had built his tomb were sealed inside along with the emperor's body. This act ensured that the tomb was safe, since no one alive would know its secrets. Hu Hai, the emperor's second son, succeeded Qin Shi Huang to the throne. He was weak, however, and lost the empire three years later to the leaders of the former kingdom of Han.

Ramses II

Egyptian pharaoh
Born c. 1315 B.C.,
Egypt
Died c. 1225 B.C.,
Egypt

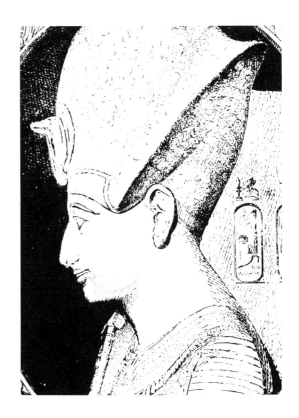

Ramses II began his reign as a warrior trying to protect the lands controlled by the great Egyptian empire. He then became a peacemaker and signed the first known peace treaty between independent powers. However, he did not achieve greatness for Egypt as a warrior or as a diplomat. Ramses sought glory as a builder. An absolute ruler, he cared more for his own undying fame than for anything else. He is often called "Ramses the Great" because of the huge monuments he had erected during his long reign. He built hundreds of them all over Egypt, more than any other pharaoh, and many of these splendid monuments exist to this day.

Ramses was the son of Seti and his wife Tuya. Since his parents were not part of the Egyptian royal family, Ramses was not directly in line to become pharaoh. This changed when he was eight years old. Pharaoh Horemheb, who had no children, named Ramses' grandfather, Pramesse, his successor. When Pramesse died after ruling only two years, Ramses' father became Seti I, the new pharoah.

"He is often called 'Ramses the Great' because of the huge monuments he had erected during his long reign."

During Seti's reign, the Egyptian empire was attacked by Libyans, Nubians (from the ancient state of Nubia in northeast Africa), and Hittites (an ancient people from Syria). Ramses began following his father into battle when he was only 15. Two years later, he was made a commander in the army and was officially declared the crown prince (next in line to the throne). He then married Nefertari, who remained his favorite wife (it was the custom for pharaohs to marry more than one wife).

Battles Hittites at Kadesh

When his father died around 1290 B.C., Ramses became pharaoh. A few years later, he decided to attack the Syrian city of Kadesh, which the Hittites had reclaimed from the Egyptians. He led an army north to Phoenicia (roughly present-day Lebanon) and took Amurru, a city that controlled the road to Kadesh. The Hittites, however, learned of Ramses' movements and quickly gathered an army to oppose him. As he moved toward the city, Ramses divided his army into four divisions. Not knowing the large number of Hittites hidden behind the walls of the city, Ramses approached with only two divisions. Hittite chariots charged forth in a surprise attack, scattering the Egyptians. Rallying his troops, Ramses managed to hold off the Hittites. The remaining divisions soon arrived, but the Hittites still outnumbered the Egyptians. The battle ended in a draw and Ramses returned to Egypt without control of Kadesh.

Despite this outcome, Ramses had monuments built with relief carvings and inscriptions describing the battle of Kadesh as a great victory. He soon had hosts of workers busy all over Egypt building monuments to honor both him and the Egyptian gods. He even had his name written on monuments built by earlier pharaohs. Among the many projects in the early years of his reign was the completion of a hall of 134 columns on the Temple of Amon-Ra (ancient Egypt's supreme god) at Karnak. This temple still stands today.

The major feature of the monuments built under Ramses is their size. At a monument in Tanis, an ancient city in the

Nile delta in northern Egypt, workers constructed a 90-foot figure of Ramses. His mortuary (funeral) temple in western Thebes, called the Ramesseum, is a complex fortress-palace. Inside, huge columns are engraved with details of his various battles against the Libyans and others.

Builds Huge Temple at Abu Simbel

The largest and most famous of Ramses' monuments is the temple he had built around 1250 B.C. at Abu Simbel, a site on the west bank of the Nile near the present-day southern border of Egypt. Here, workers cut out of the sandstone cliffs four identical figures of the seated pharaoh. These massive statues measure 67 feet high and 25 feet wide at the shoulders. They each weigh about 1,200 tons. The interior of the temple, with many halls containing more oversized statues of Ramses, penetrates 185 feet into the solid rock. During the 1960s, the Egyptian government built a dam on the Nile north of this site that threatened to flood the entire area. To save the temple, the government cut it into 950 blocks and reconstructed it on a cliff 200 feet above the river.

Almost 20 years after the battle of Kadesh, Ramses and the Hittite ruler Hattushilis signed a peace treaty. They agreed to respect each other's territories and pledged to help each other if attacked by an outside power. Ramses never broke the treaty while he was pharaoh. To secure good relations with the Hittite king, Ramses married one of his daughters. When she died seven years later, he renewed the treaty by marrying her younger sister.

Egypt remained at peace during the final years of Ramses' long reign. As he increased the splendor of the empire through his monuments, he increased the use of slaves to have them built. Upon his death, Ramses was buried in his mortuary temple with 20 treasure-filled rooms. Over the centuries, thieves broke into his tomb and stole most of his treasures. Finally, after his temple had been rediscovered in the late 1800s, his mummy and the few remaining treasures were moved to the Cairo Museum in Egypt.

Léopold Sédar Senghor

*Poet, philosopher,
and first president of Senegal*

*Born October 9, 1906,
Joal, Senegal, French West Africa*

*"Senghor never gave up
his vision of a world
free from racism,
economic inequality,
and nationalism."*

A European-educated poet who became an African politician, Léopold Sédar Senghor championed not only African independence but African culture. He helped remove French control over Senegal and became that country's first president. His greatest goal, however, was to try to join with his African neighbors while still maintaining a link to France. Although other leaders in Africa refused to accept his ideas, Senghor continued to work for African unity during the 20 years he led Senegal. He never gave up his vision of a world free from racism, economic inequality, and nationalism (the belief that one's nation or culture is superior to all others).

The son of a wealthy trader of the Serer tribe, Senghor was born in the city of Joal in 1906. Senegal was then a part of the French colony called French West Africa, which had been established in 1895. When he was eight years old, Senghor enrolled in a Roman Catholic mission school. Ten years later, hoping to become a priest, he entered a seminary in Dakar, the capital of French West Africa. For protesting against racism in the seminary, he was dismissed in 1926. Senghor then attended a public high school in Dakar, graduating with honors in 1928. Because he excelled in literature, he was given a scholarship to pursue literary studies in France—the first award of its kind to be given to an African.

Develops *Négritude* to Keep African Culture Alive

Senghor graduated from the University of Paris in 1931. Over the next two decades, he taught Latin and French language and literature to French students. During this time, along with two other black poets living in France, Senghor developed a literary movement called *négritude*. Through their poetry and other writings, the three tried to emphasize the value of African culture by showing the great influence it had on modern painting, sculpture, music, and other art forms. Followers of *négritude* also criticized European domination of Africa, which they believed led to the destruction of African culture.

When World War II began in 1939, Senghor was drafted into the French army. Captured by the Germans in 1940, Senghor spent the next two years in a Nazi concentration camp. In 1946, a year after the war ended, he was elected as a representative of Senegal to the National Assembly, the ruling legislative body of France. While in the Assembly over the next 12 years, he worked successfully for reforms in all of France's African colonies.

In the late 1950s France decided to allow its African colonies to govern themselves. Senghor tried to create an independent African Federation, grouping all of France's former west African colonies together. In 1959 he linked Senegal with French Sudan (present-day Mali) to form the Mali Federation, becoming president of the federation's legislative assembly. Because of rising nationalism in Africa, however, Senghor was unable to convince other African leaders to join his federation. In August 1960 Senegal and French Sudan separated, and Senegal became an independent republic. The people of Senegal unanimously elected Senghor the country's first president.

As president, Senghor tried to increase the economic progress of Senegal. He modernized the country's agricultural system, but a severe drought in northern Senegal in the late 1960s drastically hurt the country's economy. Throughout his term in office, Senghor spoke out against unfair trade between industrial nations and agricultural ones. To promote better trade relations and to keep his dream of a unified Africa alive, Senghor joined six other African nations in the West African Economic Community in 1974. By the late 1970s, however, many political rivals in Senegal criticized Senghor for not establishing social reforms in the country quickly enough.

In 1980, midway through his fifth term as president, Senghor resigned, devoting time to his writing. He had published his first volume of poetry, *Chants d'Ombre* (*Songs of Shadow*) in 1945, and in the succeeding years published four more volumes. All were praised by literary critics. In 1983 he was elected to the Académie Française, the most prestigious organization of scholars and writers in France. Senghor became the first black member in the Académie's 300-year history.

Siddhartha

*Better known as the Buddha,
founder of Buddhism*

*Born c. 563 B.C.
Near Kapilavastur, present-day Nepal
Died c. 483 B.C.*

S iddhartha (better known as the Buddha) is one of the most significant figures in the history of the world's great religions. Siddhartha is as important to the history and culture of Eastern civilization as Jesus (see **Jesus of Nazareth**) is to that of Western civilization. The religion he founded, Buddhism, arose in India in the sixth century B.C. and soon spread to other parts of Asia. Today over 300 million people, mainly in southeast Asia and Japan, follow the Buddha's teachings.

As with other historic religious leaders, the life of the Buddha is surrounded in legends and mystery. According to Buddhist teachings, he was born around 563 B.C. near the ancient town of Kapilavastu in present-day southern Nepal. His full name was Siddhartha Gautama. Ten months before his birth, his mother, Maya, had a dream in which a white elephant entered her womb. Seven days after Siddhartha was born, she died. His father, Suddhodana, a warrior prince, then summoned sages (wise men) to predict Siddhartha's future.

"Siddhartha is as important to the history and culture of Eastern civilization as Jesus is to that of Western civilization."

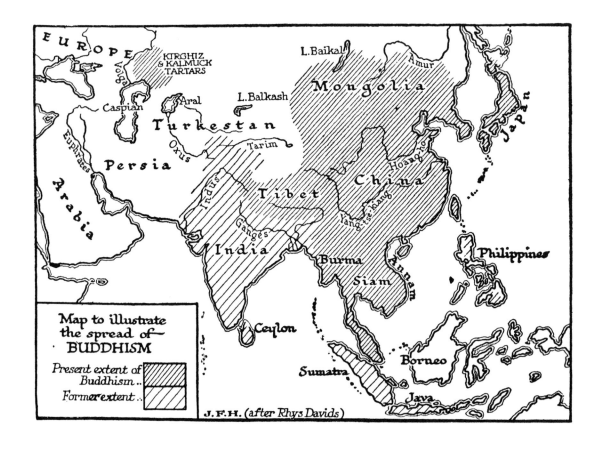

Map to illustrate the spread of BUDDHISM

Present extent of Buddhism..

Former extent..

J.F.H. (after Rhys Davids)

They prophesied (foretold) that Siddhartha would grow up to be either a king or a religious teacher. To prevent his son from following a religious life, Suddhodana raised him in luxury and sheltered him from suffering.

Changes After Seeing Misery in the World

At age 16, Siddhartha married a neighboring princess, Yasodhara, who eventually bore a son, Rahula. Curious about the outside world, Siddhartha began to take chariot rides outside of the palace walls. Legend states that on four trips he saw an old man, a sick man, a dead man, and finally a monk. These experiences exposed Siddhartha to suffering for the first time. He was overwhelmed with sorrow. At age 29, seeking a solution to end misery in the world, he left his wife and child and became a wandering monk.

To find enlightenment, Siddhartha studied yoga with two spiritual teachers. When he did not find the answers he was looking for, he began a period of fasting and self-torture. After six years of suffering, Siddhartha was still no closer to the understanding he sought. He then decided to pursue a "middle path" between the extremes of luxury and the monk's life. When he was 35 years old, he sat meditating under a bo (fig) tree one night in the village of Bodh Gaya in northeast India. In the morning, he awoke with the answers he had sought. Thereafter, he became known as the Buddha ("Enlightened One") and the tree became known as the Bodhi Tree ("Tree of Enlightenment").

The Four Noble Truths and the Eightfold Path

Through his enlightenment, Buddha became aware that life is guided by Four Noble Truths. The first is that life is full of sorrow. All living things (people, animals) suffer this sorrow over and over again as they go through a continuous cycle of death and rebirth (what Buddhists call *samsura*). The second truth is that this sorrow is brought about by desires and attachment to worldly things. The third truth is that it is possible for people to overcome their desires and the endless cycle of rebirths by reaching *nirvana,* a state of inner peace and happiness. The fourth truth is that *nirvana* can be attained by living according to the Eightfold Path. To follow this path, people must know the Four Truths, resist doing evil things, say nothing offensive to others, respect life and property, work jobs that do not hurt any living thing, have only good thoughts, pay attention to their feelings and bodies, and practice proper concentration.

For the next 45 years, Buddha preached his message, which is called the *dharma* (meaning "saving truth"). He gave his first sermon explaining the *dharma* in a park in Sarnath

---

Zen Buddhism

Zen is a school of Buddhism. Its practicies were reportedly brought to China from India by Bodhidharma in about A.D. 470. It spread to Japan in the fourteenth century. Zennists believe everyone already has inside them the awareness of the Buddha. This state of awareness cannot be reached through thinking or by following written teachings. Only through deep meditation and intuition can one attain *satori,* or enlightenment. Zen values the natural and the simple in everyday life. Through intense concentration on ordinary physical chores, Zennists express their spiritual attainment.

(ancient city in northern India) to five holy men who had been his companions. Buddha traveled primarily in northern India, attracting converts and disciples. From these followers he established a community of monks and nuns (called the *sangha*) to live and to spread the *dharma*.

Buddha continued to preach until he died around the age of 80. According to Buddhist teachings, he had reached final *nirvana*. His followers took his body, honored it with flowers, scents, and music, and then burned it. His remains were divided among eight groups of his followers, who built *stupas* (religious monuments) to house these remains. *Stupas* exist today in every country where Buddhism is practiced.

Suleiman

Sultan of the Ottoman Empire
Born c. 1494
Died September 5 (or 6), 1566

The Ottoman Empire was founded by Osman (see **Osman I**) in present-day Turkey at the beginning of the fourteenth century. Over the next two hundred years, the empire expanded to sit upon three continents—Asia, Europe, and Africa. It attained the greatest glory of its eventual 600-year history under the reign of Suleiman. He was a warrior ruler, leading his army on 13 campaigns during the 46 years he controlled the empire. He captured areas in the Mediterranean Sea and in the present-day countries of Hungary and Iraq. Suleiman was a just ruler. Because he established a new code of laws that governed the empire for the next few centuries, his Muslim subjects called him *Kanuni* ("the Lawgiver"). Because of the beautiful shrines he built on his many campaigns, European Christians called him "the Magnificent."

Suleiman was the only son of Sultan Selim I "the Grim" and Hafsa Hatun. Selim had extended the borders of the Muslim Ottoman Empire by capturing Syria and Egypt in 1517. When Suleiman succeeded his father in 1520, he continued

"The Ottoman Empire attained the greatest glory of its eventual 600-year history under the reign of Suleiman."

the tradition of conquest. From the empire's capital of Istanbul (formerly Constantinople), Suleiman marched over 100,000 of his troops northwest to the city of Belgrade (in present-day Serbia) in 1521. Sitting where the Danube and Sava rivers come together, Belgrade was the key to the defense of Christian Europe against attacks from Muslims. In just three weeks, after 20 assaults on its walls, the city fell to Suleiman. Panic swept across Europe.

The following year, Suleiman attacked another Christian stronghold, Rhodes, an island in the Aegean Sea off the west coast of present-day Turkey. The Knights Hospitalers, a Christian order of soldier-monks, had seized control of Rhodes in the early 1300s. They continually disrupted the Ottoman empire's trade between Istanbul and Egypt. Suleiman's troops lay siege to Rhodes for 145 days. In the fighting, they used bombards (cannons that hurled stones), brass guns, mortars, mines, and—for the first time in warfare—bombs. Incredibly, the Turks almost suffered defeat, but Suleiman's appearance on the battlefield rallied them. A few days before Christmas of 1522, the Knights surrendered. Suleiman let them leave Rhodes peacefully and spared the lives of the people who remained on the island.

Massacres Hungarians at Mohács

For the next three years, Suleiman did not go to war. Finally, spurred on by a desire to spread his Muslim faith, he decided to attack Hungary, controlled by the reckless boy-king Louis II. The two forces met in 1526 at Mohács, south of the present-day Budapest. Suleiman's 200,000 men massacred the 28,000 Hungarians in just two hours. Louis was drowned in the battle. This victory marked the beginning of 150 years of Ottoman control in Hungary.

In the summer of 1529, Suleiman launched his greatest threat to Christian Europe by attacking the city of Vienna in Austria. It took Suleiman and his 100,000 men 141 days to travel 1,000 miles up the Danube River from Istanbul. Vienna, a beautiful city of monasteries and churches, was ill-prepared to meet Suleiman's three-week assault. But bad weather, a lack

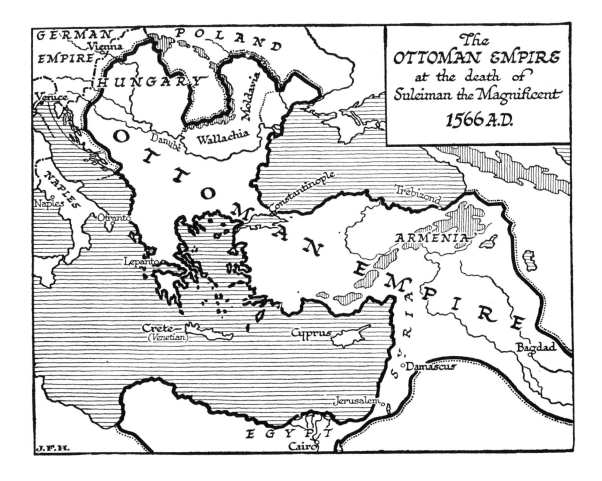

of supplies, and strong resistance by the people of Vienna forced the Ottoman Turks to withdraw. When Suleiman returned to Istanbul, however, he conducted a great celebration as if he had won.

Beginning in 1534, Suleiman waged three campaigns against neighboring Persia (present-day Iran). In the first battle, he gained control over the eastern part of Asia Minor (a peninsula forming most of present-day Turkey) and present-day Iraq. After battles in 1548 and 1554, Suleiman signed a peace treaty with Persia, adding parts of the present-day countries of Georgia and Azerbaijan to the Ottoman Empire.

Christian dominance in the Mediterranean had been threatened by Suleiman's capture of Rhodes. In response, the Spanish king Charles V (see **Charles V**), who had been crowned Holy Roman emperor, began attacking Ottoman Empire outposts in northern Africa. In 1535 he captured the Turkish stronghold at Tunis (city in present-day Tunisia). Suleiman, however, refused to give up any of his territory. His navy defeated Spanish forces off the west coast of Greece in 1538, giving him virtual control of the Mediterranean for over thirty years.

Builds Istanbul Into a Beautiful City

During his conquests, Suleiman opened up many trade routes, and merchants flooded into Istanbul. With Suleiman's strong support, the city became a center for the arts. Its gem-studded jewelry, porcelain, textiles, and carpets were admired throughout Europe. The greatest architect in Ottoman history, Sinan, worked under Suleiman. In addition to designing magnificent buildings and mosques (temples) throughout the empire, Sinan built the beautiful Suleimaniye Mosque in Istanbul in which Suleiman's body was kept after his death.

Suleiman's final years were marked by disputes among his family that ultimately led to murder. His Russian wife, Roxelana, plotted against Mustapha, Suleiman's oldest son by another woman. While on a campaign for his father in 1553, Mustapha was mysteriously strangled. When Roxelana died five years later, her two sons, Selim and Bayezid, fought for Suleiman's throne. Bayezid was defeated and fled to Persia. In exchange for money, the Persian ruler returned Bayezid and he was executed. Eight years later, while on a campaign in Hungary, Suleiman died. The Ottoman Empire had reached its limits under his rule. Selim, known as the Drunkard, succeeded Suleiman and the empire began its slow decline.

Mother Teresa

Roman Catholic missionary
Born August 27, 1910,
Skopje, Yugoslavia

Mother Teresa is among the most well-known and highly respected women in the world in the latter half of the twentieth century. In 1948 she founded a religious order of nuns in Calcutta, India, called the Missionaries of Charity. Through this order, she has dedicated her life to helping the poor, the sick, and the dying around the world, particularly those in India. Her selfless work with the needy has brought her much acclaim and many awards, including the Nobel Peace Prize in 1979.

She was born Agnes Gonxha Bojaxhiu in 1910 in Skopje, Yugoslavia (what is now Macedonia). Her parents, Nikola and Dronda Bojaxhiu, were Albanians who settled in Skopje shortly after the beginning of the century. Since her father was co-owner of a construction firm, her family lived comfortably while she was growing up. In 1928 she suddenly decided to become a nun and traveled to Dublin, Ireland, to join the Sisters of Loreto, a religious order founded in the seventeenth century. After studying at the convent for less than a year, she

"Mother Teresa has dedicated her life to helping the poor, the sick, and the dying around the world, particularly those in India"

left to join the Loreto convent in the city of Darjeeling in northeast India. On May 24, 1931, she took the name of "Teresa" in honor of St. Teresa of Avila, a sixteenth-century Spanish nun.

In 1929 Mother Teresa had been assigned to teach geography at St. Mary's High School for Girls in Calcutta, south of Darjeeling. At the time, the streets of Calcutta were crowded with beggars, lepers, and the homeless. Unwanted infants were regularly left to die on the streets or in garbage bins. On a train back to Darjeeling in 1946, Mother Teresa felt the need to abandon her position at St. Mary's to care for the needy in the slums of Calcutta. After receiving the consent of her archbishop, she began her work.

Founds the Missionaries of Charity in Calcutta

In 1948 Pope Pius XII granted Mother Teresa permission to live as an independent nun. That same year, she became an Indian citizen. After studying nursing for three months with the American Medical Missionaries in the Indian city of Patna, she returned to Calcutta to found the Missionaries of Charity. For her habit she chose a plain white sari with a blue border and a simple cross pinned to her left shoulder.

Mother Teresa initially focused her efforts on poor children in the streets, teaching them how to read and how to care for themselves. In 1949 she was joined by her first recruit, a young girl from the city of Bengal. Many of those who joined her order over the next few years were former students from St. Mary's. Each recruit was required to devote her life to serving the poor without accepting any material reward in return.

In 1952 Mother Teresa began work for which the Missionaries of Charity has been noted ever since. Her order received permission from Calcutta officials to use a portion of the abandoned temple to the goddess Kali, the Hindu goddess of death and destruction. Here Mother Teresa founded the Kalighat Home for the Dying. She and her fellow nuns gathered dying Indians off the streets of Calcutta and brought them to this home to care for them during the days before they died.

Establishes a Leper Colony

In the mid-1950s, Mother Teresa began to help victims of leprosy. The Indian government gave the Missionaries of Charity a 34-acre plot of land near the city of Asansol. Under Mother Teresa's guidance, a leper colony was established here, called Shanti Nagar (Town of Peace). For her work among the people of India, the Indian government gave her the *Padmashree* ("Magnificent Lotus") Award in September of 1962.

In 1965 Pope Paul VI placed the Missionaries of Charity directly under the control of the papacy (the office of the pope). He also authorized Mother Teresa to expand the order outside of India. Centers to treat lepers, the blind, the disabled, the aged, and the dying were soon opened worldwide, including one in Rome in 1968. Mother Teresa also organized schools and orphanages for the poor. The Brothers of Charity, the male companion to the Sisters of Charity, was formed in the mid-1960s to run the homes for the dying.

In 1971 Pope Paul VI honored Mother Teresa by awarding her the first Pope John XXIII Peace Prize. The following year the government of India presented her with the Jawaharlal Nehru Award for International Understanding. In 1979 she received her greatest award, the Nobel Peace Prize. Mother Teresa accepted all of these awards on behalf of the poor, using any money that accompanied them to fund her centers. By 1990 over 3,000 nuns belonged to the Missionaries of Charity, running centers in 25 countries.

Theodora

Byzantine empress
Born c. 500
Died 548

In 330 the Roman emperor Constantine (see **Constantine I**) founded a second Roman capital at Byzantium (site of present-day Istanbul, Turkey). In recognition of its founder, the city was named Constantinople. When Rome fell in 476, what remained of the once great Roman Empire became known as the Byzantine Empire, with Constantinople as its capital. Disputes between rival political and religious groups almost immediately threatened the existence of this empire. It was brought back to power by the emperor Justinian I, who was crowned in 527. In addition to legal reforms, great achievements in Byzantine art and architecture marked his rule. The glories of his reign, however, were not his alone. His wife, Theodora, ruled as his partner. Her intelligence and courage helped save and advance the Byzantine Empire.

Details of Theodora's early life are somewhat sketchy. While a few early historians believe she was born on the island of Crete off the southern coast of Greece, others list her birthplace as Syria. Her father, Acacius, was a bear trainer at the hippodrome in Constantinople. The hippodrome was a gigantic stadium where chariot races, circuses, and plays were held. After her father's death, Theodora began to work on the stage in the hippodrome as a mime. She soon became a full-fledged actress. At the time, "actress" was synonymous with "prostitute." On the stage, she was noted for her nude entertainment. Off the stage, she was noted for her wild parties.

Converts to Monophysitism

When she was 16, Theodora traveled to northern Africa as the companion of an official named Hecebolus. She stayed with him for almost four years before heading back to Constantinople. On the way, she settled briefly in Alexandria, the luxurious capital of Egypt. While there, she adopted the beliefs of Monophysitism. This form of Christianity held that Jesus (see **Jesus of Nazareth**) was wholly divine, not both human and divine as orthodox Christians believed. Because they went against accepted Church teachings, Monophysites were scorned by other Christians.

After her conversion to Monophysitism, Theodora gave up her former lifestyle. She returned to Constantinople in 522, settled in a house near the palace, and made a living spinning wool. It was here that she drew the attention of Justinian. He was 40 years old at the time, almost twice her age. Justinian wanted to marry her, but as heir to the throne of his uncle, Emperor Justin I, he could not. An old Roman law forbade government officials from marrying actresses. Justin finally repealed this law the following year, and Justinian and Theodora were married in 525.

On April 4, 527, Justin crowned Justinian and Theodora emperor and empress. When Justin died in August of that year, the couple assumed control of the Byzantine Empire. Although they did not officially rule as joint monarchs, they in fact did. Justinian allowed Theodora to share his throne and influence his decisions because he recognized her abilities and intelligence.

Determined Speech Saves Empire

It was during the Nika revolt that Theodora proved her leadership. Two rival political groups existed in the empire—

Blues and Greens. Disagreements over Monophysitism and orthodox Christianity had further separated them. In January 532, while staging a chariot race in the hippodrome, these two groups started a riot. They set many public buildings on fire and proclaimed a new emperor. Unable to control the mob, Justinian and many of his advisors prepared to flee. At a meeting of the government council, Theodora courageously spoke out against leaving the palace. She thought it was better to die as a ruler than to live as nothing. Her determined speech convinced all. Justinian's generals then attacked the hippodrome, killing over 30,000 rebels. Historians agree that her courage saved Justinian's crown.

Following the Nika revolt, Theodora and Justinian rebuilt Constantinople. They transformed it into the most splendid city the world saw for centuries. They built aqueducts, bridges, and more than 25 churches. The greatest of these is the Hagia Sophia, Church of the Holy Wisdom. It is considered to be one of the architectural wonders of the world. Its dome measures 108 feet in diameter and its crown rises 180 feet above the ground. Rich marbles and mosaics of emerald green, rose, white, blood red, black, and silver decorate its walls. In the fifteenth century it became an Islamic mosque; today it is a museum.

Theodora influenced Justinian's legal and spiritual reforms. She had laws passed that prohibited forced prostitution and that granted women more rights in divorce cases. She also established homes for prostitutes. Even though Justinian supported orthodox Christianity, Theodora continued to follow Monophysitism. She provided shelter in the palace for Monophysite leaders and founded a Monophysite monastery in Sycae, across the harbor from Constantinople. After her death, Justinian worked to find harmony between the Monophysites and the orthodox Christians in the empire.

Theodora died of cancer on June 28, 548. Her body was buried in the Church of the Holy Apostles, one of the splendid churches the emperor and empress had built in Constantinople. Both Theodora and Justinian are represented in beautiful mosaics that exist to this day in the church of San Vitale at Ravenna in northern Italy, which was completed a year before her death.

Zenobia

Palmyrene warrior queen
Ruled 267-272

She was strong, beautiful, intelligent, and courageous. She also may have been murderous. It is impossible to know the full truth about Bat Zabbai—better known as Queen Zenobia. Most of what is known about her took place in the five years she led Palmyra, an ancient city in what is now the country of Syria. During that time, Zenobia tried to free Palmyra from the rule of the Roman Empire—and tried to widen her own rule. She conquered lands that the Romans claimed to own and refused to bow to their leaders. For this she fought bravely, but unsuccessfully, against the Empire.

The facts of Zenobia's life during her five-year rule come from the written histories of those she opposed, the Romans. Details on the rest of her life have been passed down through legends—stories told among Zenobia's people, who over the years may have adorned the truth in order to relate the spirit of the warrior queen.

One such legend of Zenobia's life describes her childhood. She was born of Arabic descent to a great desert-chief

"Her defiance of the Roman Empire set an example for other leaders, and her legend grew."

named Antiochus, who had many wives and children. In Antiochus's view, the only benefit to having daughters was their role in sealing treaties with neighboring tribes through arranged marriages. Since there was no such need when Zenobia was born, her father tried to get rid of her. But Zenobia was hidden away and raised with the boys in the household. According to legend, this was how she learned to hunt and to kill, and how she developed great physical strength.

To understand Zenobia's life, one must understand Palmyra's history at the time. For centuries, Palmyra was an important Middle Eastern trade center. With a safe road running through the city, goods could be bought and sold there easily. Traders and merchants came from as far away as Rome in the west and the Persian Gulf in the east. Recognizing how important Palmyra was, Rome made it part of the Roman Empire in 114.

Just over a hundred years later, the Roman Empire started to lose control of some of its colonies. Many of its emperors died unexpectedly. Rome could not manage the far reaches of its empire, and Palmyra soon took charge of its own affairs. At that time, Septimius Odainat became the city's uncrowned king. After fighting with the Empire in its war with Persia (now known as Iran), Odainat was made Palmyra's Roman consul, or governing official. But Odainat chose instead the title "King of Kings," and Rome did not object.

Many Believe Zenobia a Murderer

Odainat ruled over Palmyra with increasing power. He planned on having his son, Hairan, take over his rule. In 267, however, Odainat and Hairan were both murdered. Odainat's nephew Maeonis was charged with committing the double murder, but many thought Odainat's wife—Zenobia—was responsible. Some believed Zenobia was guilty because her young son from a previous marriage, Vaballath, was now heir to the throne. Others believed Zenobia wanted the throne for herself. Neither her guilt nor her innocence has ever been proven.

As queen, being married to Odainat, Zenobia acquired great wealth. She also had many advisors and tutors. She studied Greek and Roman authors and could speak five lan-

Cities of ASIA MINOR, SYRIA & MESOPOTAMIA
during the first centuries
of the Christian Era....

Trade routes ----
Mountains shaded
vertically.

J.F.H.

guages—Arabic, Greek, Aramaic, Egyptian, and Latin. Some felt that with her riches and vast knowledge Zenobia would easily take over the rule.

The Roman emperor Gallienus declared the boy-king Vaballath as rightful heir and Zenobia as his regent (the person who would rule in Vaballath's place until he came of age). In 268, the new emperor, Claudius, reversed this decision. But upon Claudius's sudden death, Emperor Aurelian recognized Vaballath as heir. Aurelian had coins hammered with Vaballath's portrait on one side and his own on the other. Zenobia, however, was determined that she, not Aurelian, would rule the region with her son. In 269 she sent her chief general Zabdas to attack Egypt, one of the Empire's richest territories. By 270 Egypt belonged to Zenobia and the Palmyrene kingdom.

Zenobia Insults Roman Empire

The following year, Zenobia captured the city of Antioch in what is now Turkey. There the queen stopped the production of coins bearing the emperor's name. In their place, she had coins made with her name one one side and Vaballath's on the other. This was an extreme insult to the Roman Empire. It was as if she had declared war. Aurelian sent his general Probus to recapture Egypt while he went after Zenobia.

Aurelian chased Zenobia east to the city of Tyana. Before Aurelian attacked the city, Tyana's famous philosopher, Appolonius, reportedly appeared to Aurelian in ghostly form, warning him not to harm the city. Aurelian obeyed, and Zenobia was able to escape back to Antioch. Battles were fought in Antioch and then at the city of Emesa, where Zenobia's army was badly beaten. She and Zabdas escaped back to Palmyra, 100 miles away. Aurelian soon followed and, surrounding the city, demanded that Zenobia surrender. She refused. As he attacked the city, Zenobia escaped to seek help from Persia. But while trying to cross the Euphrates River, she was captured.

Zenobia's and Zabdas's lives were spared at their trial; the lives of her other close advisors were not. Aurelian was granted a triumphant entry through the gates of Rome. Chariots, wild beasts, leopards, elephants, prisoners, and gladiators were paraded through the streets. Zenobia was also paraded, a prize catch, decorated with so many gems and so much gold she could hardly walk. Afterward, it is believed, Zenobia settled well into Roman life, even marrying a Roman senator. But her defiance of the Roman Empire set an example for other leaders, and her legend grew.

Zhao Kuang-yin

Founder of China's Song dynasty

Born 927,
Lo Yang, in present-day Honan, China

Died 976,
K'ai Feng, in present-day Honan

Zhao Kuang-yin (Chao K'uang-yin) was the first emperor of the Song (Sung) dynasty, which ruled China for over 300 years. When he became emperor, Zhao unified China, putting an end to many years of warfare between regions. He usurped the throne (took it by force), the last emperor in Chinese history to do so, but did not use the resources of his country for his own gain. Instead, under his and other Song governments, China became more prosperous than it had been under any previous dynasty. Achievements in economy, technology, and culture placed China ahead of all other countries in the world during that time. Zhao's reign set the standard for the Song dynasty, known as one of the most magnificent periods in Chinese history.

Zhao Kuang-yin was born in 927 in the city of Lo Yang in the present-day province of Honan. His father, a general in the army, trained him to be a professional soldier. While Zhao grew up, he watched the country suffer through disunity and warfare. After the T'ang dynasty ended in 907, China fell into

> *"Zhao's reign set the standard for the Song dynasty, known as one of the most magnificent periods in Chinese history."*

a half century of civil war known as the Five Dynasties and Ten Kingdoms period. In the area previously ruled by the central government, ten dominant kingdoms arose controlled by corrupt officials and army commanders. Warfare between these kingdoms ravaged the countryside. During this period, five emperors tried to govern the country, but they were all weak and short-lived.

The last emperor of this period, Shi Zong, trusted Zhao and appointed him the chief commander of the capital armies. Shi Zong died in 959, leaving a seven-year-old son as his heir. In a country already torn apart by war, the people were alarmed by the thought of a child leader. The following year, the army declared Zhao the new emperor and marched to the capital city of Kai Feng. When Zhao arrived at the palace, he forced the boy emperor from the throne, but did so without bloodshed.

Conquers Ten Warring Kingdoms

Two urgent problems faced Zhao and his Song administration: how to unify the country and how to strengthen the government to prevent anyone else from taking the throne. He decided to attack the southern kingdoms first, which were prosperous but had weak armies. In hopes of maintaining their independence, some of these wealthy kingdoms sent priceless treasures to Zhao. He responded with both kindness and force. When southern kings came to his court seeking a meeting, he gently but firmly told them to surrender their territory. Knowing they could not defeat him in battle, they pledged their allegiance. Other kings who held out against him soon faced his superior troops. During Zhao's reign, the ten kingdoms either surrendered or were conquered one by one.

Most civilians were not harmed during these conquests. To ensure that no more violence or warfare took place in China, Zhao established a strong national army. He first persuaded the high-ranking generals of the former kingdoms to give up their positions and to return to their hometowns. In exchange, he rewarded them with lands and riches. The armies of the former kingdoms were then placed under the national army, which was controlled directly by Zhao. Regions could no longer battle each other since only one army existed in China.

Under Zhao, the empire became more thoroughly centralized or concentrated than ever before in Chinese history. He set up a government that allowed him personal control over its various branches. All administrators were directly responsible to the emperor. Zhao also developed a system to expose the abuse of power among his administrators. He had certain officials monitor the activities of all administrators, including high-ranking ones. When Zhao's top advisor, Zhao Pu, committed some illegal acts and it was brought to the emperor's attention, he angrily fired Zhao Pu.

Encourages Intellectual Freedom During His Rule

Though Zhao was not a scholar, he had a high regard for those who were. He tried to fill government positions with intellectuals and even supervised the civil service examinations in person. Because these officials were chosen directly by Zhao, they were grateful and remained loyal to him. Zhao permitted other intellectuals who were not part of the government to engage openly in political discussions, even if these discussions raised criticisms of his government.

Unlike previous emperors, Zhao often left the palace and moved freely among the common people. He encouraged high government officials and the many empresses in the palace to reject luxury. One story from the period relates how the emperor demanded that the curtains for his house be made not of silk and satin but of grey cotton. He managed China's economy fairly, and both internal and external trade flourished. Zhao died at Kai Feng in 976, a year after the last of the ten kingdoms submitted to his government. He left a reunified and stable country to his successors in the Song dynasty.

Zoroaster

Ancient Persian prophet,
founder of Zoroastrianism

Born c. 588 B.C.
Died c. 511 B.C.

"Zoroaster wandered the deserts of Persia preaching a new religion based on one god who oversaw the struggle between good and evil."

When Cyrus the Great (see **Cyrus II, the Great**) was forming the Persian Empire, numerous religions existed in Persia (present-day Iran). Led by priests and wizards, many of these religions included animal sacrifices. Almost all involved the worship of a number of gods or animal spirits. These beliefs were challenged by the prophet or holy man Zoroaster (also known as Zarathustra). He wandered the deserts of Persia preaching a new religion based on one god who oversaw the struggle between good and evil. His beliefs soon spread throughout the Persian Empire, becoming the accepted faith of its kings. This religion, known as Zoroastrianism, has lasted for centuries. The Parsis, members of a religious community in India, still follow Zoroaster's teachings.

What is known about Zoroaster comes from legends. Scholars believe he was born sometime in the late sixth century B.C. (some say even earlier) in present-day northeastern Iran. His father, Pourushaspa, may have been related to the Persian royal family. His mother, Dughdhova, was the daughter of a minor Persian nobleman. Many extraordinary events are linked to Zoroaster's life. Legend states that while he was in his mother's womb, she gave off light. When he was born, Zoroaster did not cry, but simply smiled and laughed.

Has Visions of a God

At the age of 30, while drawing water at the edge of a river, Zoroaster had his first religious vision. A large spirit led his soul into the heavens where he met a god, whom he called Ahura Mazda. Over a series of eight visions, this god instructed Zoroaster in the Good Religion, what came to be known as Zoroastrianism.

According to Zoroaster's teachings, Ahura Mazda is the supreme god who created all things and is righteous and holy. Surrounding him are six attendants or good spirits. Leading the evil spirits of the world is Ahriman, the god of darkness and lies. A great struggle takes place in the world between Spenta Mainyu, a good spirit, and Angra Mainyu, an evil one. Ahura Mazda calls upon people to aid Spenta Mainyu in this battle by living a life filled with good thoughts and good deeds. Upon their deaths, people are then rewarded by Ahura Mazda according to how well they fought in the battle against evil. Zoroaster wrote these beliefs into several hymns called the *Gathas*. Centuries later, these hymns and other writings were gathered into the Zoroastrian bible, the *Avesta*.

Persian King Helps Spread Zoroastrianism

Zoroaster wandered Persia for almost ten years preaching this new religion to its people before he came upon Vishtaspa, the king of an important eastern Persian state. When Zoroaster arrived in the king's court, the resident priests challenged his beliefs for three days. Zoroaster's ability to read the king's mind, however, greatly impressed Vishtaspa. As a result, the priests accused Zoroaster of being a sorcerer and threw him into prison. Vishtaspa's favorite black stallion then became ill—its legs drew up beneath its body and it could not move. Zoroaster promised to save the horse if the king, his wife, and his son accepted and spread the Good Religion. Once the king readily agreed, the stallion returned to perfect health.

Vishtaspa's kingdom quickly adopted Zoroastrianism after the king's conversion. Zoroaster spent almost the next forty years spreading his beliefs throughout the rest of the Persian Empire. Even though he gained many disciples willing to carry his message, a few people in the empire still clung to the old religions. One of these was a priest named Turi-Bratar-Vakhsh. According to the *Avesta,* this priest encountered Zoroaster while the 77-year-old prophet was conducting a fire ceremony at the alter of Balkh (fire is considered by Zoroastrians to be a sign of the truth of Ahura Mazda). There, within the sanctuary, Turi-Bratar-Vakhsh killed Zoroaster.

After Zoroaster's death, his religion thrived in Persia for centuries. It also spread beyond the bounds of the empire. The symbol of Zoroastrianism, the winged god Ahura Mazda, decorated fire temples and palaces from present-day India west to the Mediterranean Sea. Perhaps the most famous Zoroastrians in ancient times were the Magi, the three wise men in the New Testament of the Bible who journeyed to Bethlehem to witness the birth of Jesus (see **Jesus of Nazareth**). Although small in number, the Parsis keep this religion alive today, reading from the *Avesta* and attending fire rituals.

Picture Credits

Photographs and illustrations appearing in *World Leaders: People Who Shaped the World* were received from the following sources:

Courtesy of Chester Beatty Library, Dublin: volume 1: p. 4; **courtesy of Chinese Information Service:** volume 1: p. 14; **AP/Wide World Photos:** volume 1: pp. 37, 99; **courtesy of the USSR State Archival Fund:** volume 2: p. 256; **courtesy of Caisse Nationale des Monuments Historiques et des Sites, Paris:** volume 2: p. 260; **courtesy of the Organization of American States:** timeline; volume 3: pp. 342, 471, 496; **courtesy of the John F. Kennedy Library,** photo no. AR6283A: timeline; volume 3: p. 391; **courtesy of Franklin D. Roosevelt Library:** volume 3: pp. 442, 447.

Master Index

Boldface indicates profiles

Appomattox Courthouse 378, 408, 414
Aquitaine 201, 202, 204, 249
Arab–Israeli War 90
Aragon 239–241
Arapaho 359, 455, 457
Arawak 471, 472
Arbenz Guzmán, Jacobo 381
Armada (Spanish) 207, 208
Articles of Confederation 490
The Art of Courtly Love 203
Ashurbanipal 7–9
Assyrian Empire 7, 9
Astyages 24, 25
Aswan High Dam 91, 92
Atahualpa 192
Attila the Hun 165–167
August Coup 224
Augustus 20, **168–171**, 175, 198
Aurelian 133, 134
Austerlitz, battle of 286
Aztec 189, 191, 430–433

B

Babar 4
Babylon 8, 9, 25, 26, 47, 49
Babylonia 8, 24, 25, 47–49
Balfour Declaration 11
Bandar Abbas 3
Bannockburn, battle of 302
Barnett, Samuel 336
Batista, Fulgencio 381, 382
Batu Khan 290
Bay of Pigs Invasion 394
Beer–hall putsch 235
Belgrade, battle of 122
Ben–Gurion, David 10–13
Berlin Wall 224, 394
The Bible 64, 65, 67, 82–84, 140, 436
Black Hawk War 410
Black Hills 358, 359, 457
Black Muslims 416–418
Bloomer, Amelia 339

The Bloudy Tenent of Persecution for the Cause of Conscience 494
Bo tree 119
Bodh Gaya 119
Boers 313
Bohemia 305
Bolívar, Simón 342–345, 454
Bolsheviks 257, 258
Booth, John Wilkes 414
Bothwell, James Hepburn 280
Bourgeoisie 276, 277
Boyars 245, 246
Bozeman Trail 358, 456
Bozeman, John 358, 456
Bradford, William 346–349
Brandenburg 216, 217, 219, 220
Breitenfeld 231
Breitenfeld, Battle of 231
Brezhnev, Leonid 222
Brock, Isaac 470
Brown, John 364, 406, 481
Brown v. *Board of Education* 397, 421
Buddha (see Siddhartha)
Buddhism 117, 120
Bull Run, battles of 407, 412
Bursa 103
Byzantine Empire 61–63, 101–103, 128–130, 187, 198, 225, 227, 296, 309

C

Caesar, Julius 19, 168, 169, **172–175,** 184, 198
Camisards 402
Canaan 84
Cannae, battle of 52
Canute I, the Great 176–179, 271
Capitalism 254, 276
Carranza, Venustiano 498
Carthage 50, 52
Castile 239–241, 243

Herzl, Theodor 11
Hinduism 5, 6, 35, 96
Hispaniola 471–473
Historical materialism 276, 277
History of Plymouth Plantation 348
History of Woman Suffrage 340, 465
Hitler, Adolf 12, **233–238,** 450, 451
Hittites 112, 113
Ho Chi Minh 57–60
Ho Chi Minh City 60
Hohenzollern 216, 220
Holocaust 12
Holy Roman Empire 190, 213, 214, 231, 233, 282, 286, 294, 295, 308
Hoover, Herbert 449
House of Commons 194–196
Howard, Oliver Otis 354
Huerta, Victoriano 498
Huguenots 262
Huitzilopochtli 431, 432
Hull House 335–337
Humanism 206
Humayun 4–6
Hundred Days battle 288
Hundred Years War 249
Hunkpapa Sioux 359, 455–457
Huns 165–167, 294
Hussein, Saddam 74

I

Iconoclasm 62
"I Have a Dream" speech 399
Imperialism 34, 57, 313
Inca 189, 192
India Act of 1935 37
Indian National Congress 36, 37, 94, 96
Indochina 57–59
Indulgences 265, 266
Industrial Revolution 57, 275, 335

Instruction 182
Iran hostage crisis 71, 73
Iran–Iraq War 74
Irene of Athens 61–63
Isabella I 189, **239–243**
Isfahan 1, 3
Istanbul 122, 124
Italian Wars 190
Ivan IV, the Terrible 244–247

J

Jackson, Thomas J. "Stonewall" 407, 408
Jacobins 283
Jahangir 6
Jamestown 459–461
Jamukha 40, 41
Jefferson, Thomas 373, **384-387,** 490
Jen 23
Jesus of Nazareth 64–67, 85, 117, 129, 140, 214, 402
Jim Crow laws 366, 485
Joan of Arc 248–251
John XXIII 252–255
Johnson, Lyndon 395
Johnston, Joseph E. 407
Juana Inés de la Cruz 388–390
Judas Iscariot 67
Justin I 129
Justinian I 128–130

K

Kaaba 86, 87
Kadesh, battle of 112, 113
Kai Feng 136, 137
Kalmar Union 273
Kampaku 32, 33
Kansas–Nebraska Act 410
Karnak 55, 112
Kennedy, John F. 391–395, 417, 421
Kenyan African National Union 70
Kenyan African Union 69

Mein Kampf 235, 237
Melbourne, William 311
Mendive, Rafael María de 422, 423
Menelik II 43
Mensheviks 257
Mesopotamia 47, 48
Metacomet 495
Metaurus River, battle of 52
Mexican Revolution 496–499
Mexican War 376, 378, 406
Middle Ages 1, 185, 201, 203, 214, 264, 316
Miles, Nelson 355, 359
Miranda, Francisco de 343
Missionaries of Charity 125–127
Missouri Compromise 410
Moctezuma II 192, **430–432**
Mohács, battle of 122
Mongols 4, 39, 40, 42, 101, 102, 289–292
Monophysitism 129, 130
Montgomery bus boycott 396, 397
Montgomery Improvement Association 397
Monts, Pierre du Gua de 351, 352
Moors 242
Moses 64, **82–85**
Mott, Lucretia 464
Mount Vernon 488, 491
Mughal Empire 4–6
Muhammad 12, **85–88,** 417
Muhammad Reza Shah Pahlevi 71–73
Muhammad, Elijah 416, 417
Muslim League 37
Muslim Mosque, Inc. 417
Mussolini, Benito 43, 45

N

NAACP (see National Association for the Advancement of Colored People)

Nabonidus 25
Naguib, Muhammad 91
Napoleon I Bonaparte 282–288, 342, 453, 473
Narragansett 494
Narrative of Sojourner Truth 475, 477
Nasser, Gamal Abdal 89–92
National American Woman Suffrage Association 340, 465
National Assembly 115, 283, 472
National Association for the Advancement of Colored People 367, 369, 419, 420, 421
National Convention 283, 436
National Federation of Settlements and Neighborhood Centers 337
National Industrial Recovery Act 450
National Negro Business League 485
National Woman Suffrage Association 340, 465
National Youth Administration 445
Natural rights 464, 465
Nazis 12, 195, 235, 236, 253, 450
Nebuchadnezzar 26
Necho 8
Négritude 115
Nehru, Jawaharlal 93-96
Nelson, Horatio 285
Nevsky, Alexander 289–292
New Deal 442, 445, 447, 449, 450
New Economic Policy 259
New France 350, 351
New Granada 342
Newport, Christopher 460, 461
New Spain 342, 388
Nez Percé 353–356
Niagara Movement 367
Nicaea, Second Council of 62

William the Conqueror 314–317
Williams, Roger 492–495
Wilson, Woodrow 448
Wingfield, Edward 460
Woman Suffrage Movement 337–340, 361, 365, 463–466, 481
The Woman's Bible 465
Women's International League for Peace and Freedom 337
Women's Loyal League 340
Women's Peace Party 337
Works Progress Administration (WPA) 450
World Anti–Slavery Convention 464
World War I 11, 36, 58, 97, 234, 253, 258, 337
World War II 12, 17, 37, 43, 58, 80, 95, 96, 115, 195, 196, 237, 391, 445, 447, 450

X

Xian Yang 108, 109

Y

Yeltsin, Boris 224
Yorktown, battle of 489

Z

Zama, battle of 52
Zanzibar 97, 98
Zapata, Emiliano 496–498
Zapatistas 497–499
Zemski Sobor 245
Zen Buddhism 119
Zeno of Citium 269
Zenobia 131–134, 197
Zhao Kuang–yin 135–137
Zionism 10, 11
Zoroaster 138–140
Zoroastrianism 6, 138–140